Praise for
Treasures of Scouting

"Many people have talked of the importance of the scouting program, but until now no one has specifically told us how to create a program that works. This one-of-kind book by Jeff Johnson explains exactly how to do it. It will equip you with examples of how to create a scouting program that has purpose and will help young men accomplish wonders in every aspect of their life."

—*Wayne John, Retired Educator*

The Treasures of Scouting transported me back to my youth, bringing back memories of friendships made, lessons learned, and goals met. I highly recommend this book, which offers an inside look into the great benefits that come to all who participate in the programs of the Boy Scouts of America."

—*Gregory C. Schaelling, Lieutenant Colonel (Retired), USAF, and Eagle Scout*

THE TREASURES
of SCOUTING
Character Traits and Skills to Ensure Youth Success

By

Jeff Johnson

The Treasures of Scouting
Copyright © 2016 Jeff Johnson

Design by
Arbor Books, Inc.
www.arborbooks.com

Printed in the United States of America

The Treasures of Scouting
Jeff Johnson

1. Title   2. Author   3. Adventure

Library of Congress Control Number: 2016904978
ISBN: 978-0-692-67514-4

Dedication

First of all, I want to dedicate this work to my wife, Julie, and my family for supporting me in the many responsibilities I've had toward the Boy Scouts over the years.

Contents

Special Thanks

In addition, I want to thank the many good friends (George Gettys, Steve Brown, Sam Martinez, Jody Wood, Patrick Hoggan, Ken Hazelbaker, Brian Matthews, Dean Thompson, Brad Anderson, and Gary McFadyen) in California who encouraged, supported, trained, and served with me in many of the responsibilities I had with the Boy Scouts of America. They have become dear friends. If it weren't for the time I spent in California, I never would have discovered how important scouting really is and what a program should look like. It was because of this time that I discovered the many treasures of scouting.

Introduction

Have you ever failed to completely appreciate a situation or a relationship until the situation or relationship was gone? That's happened to me many times; you would have thought I would have learned after the first couple of times. My grandfather was the first person with whom I took a relationship for granted, and I didn't realize that's what I was doing until it was too late. As a little boy, I would visit my grandfather in McGill, Nevada, several times a year. Since my grandparents lived so far away, we usually stayed for a week or two when we visited, unless it was during the school year.

We went to their house almost every Thanksgiving weekend. One tradition that was part of that weekend was to travel up into the mountains to cut down a Christmas tree. During the summer, the town of McGill had a swimming pool (though it was more like a pond with a lifeguard) where we loved to play. It was fed from a stream, so the pool had fish in it. Near the bank were schools of minnows that were fun to catch and put in a jar. My grandfather would take us camping in the mountains and make us whistles from willow branches.

After high school and into college, my life became busy (as far as I was concerned). When my family went to visit my grandparents, I made excuses for why I couldn't go. One day while I was at school doing some homework, a friend of mine found me and said that he needed to take me home because my grandfather had passed away. I couldn't believe it; my grandfather wasn't that old and I wasn't ready for him to be out of my life. Before that day, I had thought I had all the time in the world to see him. I should have treasured that relationship better.

In *The Seven Habits of Highly Effective People*, Stephen Covey explains how relationships are like bank accounts: If you want your relationships to be valuable, you need to make more deposits than withdrawals. A deposit in a relationship is doing something good for a person; a withdrawal is the opposite. I suppose my relationship with my grandfather was overdrawn, since he definitely made more deposits than I did. I think for many people, it's hard to see a situation when they're in the middle of it.

When I lived in California, I certainly didn't comprehend the significance of where I lived, who my friends were, or what the scouting environment was giving me. I want to give others an idea about how I came to realize how fortunate I was. Shortly after my family and I moved to California, I was asked to serve in scouting. I was introduced to some seriously dedicated adult volunteer scouters. It was curious to me to see volunteers so dedicated and hardworking for a program. At my family's first day at church, we were invited to a potluck dinner. George Gettys and his family were there. At the time, George was part of the congregation leadership and a former scout leader. When I was asked to be the team coach for fourteen- and fifteen-year-old boys for the troop the very next weekend, I suspected he was the reason. Shortly after that, he was released from his leadership position and made the scout master. We've been on more than one hundred campouts together. He's probably the best friend I've ever had.

The troop in the Sacramento area was sponsored by a religious organization that provided funds and staffing. One of the things I remember is the significant support of the leadership at all levels. The congregation we attended is also known as a ward. The church has many levels of leadership starting from the congregational (several hundred members) to the stake (up to a dozen congregations) and to the area or region (dozens of stakes). At least one member of our stake leadership would attend Philmont Scout Ranch or the Wood Badge training course every year and encourage at least one adult scout member of each ward to do the same at the expense of the stake.

The scouting program in our ward was well supported by our local leadership, who made sure we had enough volunteers and funds to run the scouting program. When we had scout activities away from our church building, many parents would often attend. Shortly after I was asked to be a unit leader, two other men were called to be unit leaders and they became close friends. We all had been trained at Wood Badge and remained in that troop as unit leaders for almost eight years, although we were moved around within the troop to different unit leader positions. We usually ran the unit weekday activities separately, but all the significant monthly activities were done together. I'm sure you can imagine how close we became as friends after spending so much time together.

Most of the volunteers on the troop committee were parents of scouts in the program. Committee meetings were held at least once a month, and the committee functioned as designated by the BSA, allowing the unit leaders to focus their efforts on the quality operation of the troop. In addition, youth participants received Junior Leader Training in order to be significantly engaged in leadership responsibilities designated by the BSA.

After thirteen years of living in California, I had to move back to Utah to attend to my ailing mother. I lamented not being in California, working in that scouting organization. If ever there was a perfectly running scout program, it had to have been the troop I worked for in Citrus Heights, California.

I thought a lot about the differences between the BSA programs I had been in and made mental notes. After having a couple of hours each morning for personal reflection, I decided I was going to make a list of all the great benefits I received during my time serving in scouts. I began to spend an hour or so each morning contemplating the activities I had been on, the things I had learned, or things I had seen the boys learn as a result of the program.

As the list got larger and larger, I wanted to put a title to it. I settled on *The Treasures of Scouting* because it described the way I really felt about the list. A treasure can be a desirable trait, characteristic, skill, or amount of knowledge that magnifies one's likelihood of success or happiness; it is a memorable experience so powerful that it will not be forgotten.

I felt inspired to write this book, that perhaps it might encourage more participation in the BSA programs. This book is an accumulation of some of my most treasured experiences in scouting, and shares information from those experiences. I've also included information from studies done by Baylor University and the BSA that definitively show that young men who participate in scouting acquire most of the traits that are desirable for young men to have. Furthermore, studies show a decline in traditional values in America; the US military even believes we are on a collision course with failure, according to some studies. I believe the BSA holds the key to reverse this trend.

When I was first asked to be a scout leader, I was young and newly married. I was working, going to school for electrical engineering, and had little free time. I didn't comprehend as a young kid with little knowledge or experience in scouting how important and what an impact scouting has on young men. Over the years, as I learned more and received more training, the scouting program ran better and better. The more time I spent and learned, the more I appreciated. Even after decades of time, I still didn't truly comprehend how significant the BSA programs really were. I would like to impart that significance to you.

Value Incorporation

During my years in scouting, I have seen the effect it has on young men and how it strengthens their character. A study done by three master's students at Baylor University from 2012 entitled "Eagle Scouts Merit beyond the Badge" indicated various characteristics that the BSA develops in the lives of the young men who participate. The more the young men surveyed in the study were involved, the stronger those character influences were expressed in their lives. "The programs of the BSA are designed to incorporate activities and learning experiences that strengthen young people's attitudes and actions toward God, family, country, and community. Ultimately, the aim of BSA programs has been . . . positive and robust influence on the character, citizenship, and physical fitness of youth who participate."

The study summarized forty-four general traits, which I've listed at the end of the book. The table is by no means a complete list and is actually a small part of my research, but it summarizes the improvements in young men due to the BSA programs. What parents wouldn't want their child to participate in such a program? What community leader wouldn't want to have youth participate in scouting? Scouting will hopefully counteract the declining values of society. Overall, the study indicated that a scout is more probable to be successful and happy in life due to the skills and traits acquired from scouting. Please see the suggestions for further reading also. My research groups the positive influences of scouting into three main areas: value incorporation, good decision making, and self-discovery. In this first section, I'll provide some examples that illustrate some of these values.

Bravery

One Saturday in the winter of 1994, our church organization planned a sleigh-riding trip to a popular location that served as a golf course in the summer. The clubhouse was open to provide warmth and food. After a couple of hours of sleigh riding, it started to snow. Within a few short minutes, it became a whiteout so severe that I couldn't see more than ten to twenty feet in front of me. Our church leaders were concerned about getting all the participants safely back up the hill, especially the kids. They tried to make assignments quickly for adults to comb the mountain and rescue those who might have been struggling to get to safety.

A couple of the young men with whom I had worked in scouting stepped forward and volunteered to assist. After I returned to the clubhouse from my own part of the search, I became concerned for those still outside, especially those young men. I had taken a cold weather awareness course and understood the seriousness of this situation. Eventually, most of the searchers returned, but one young man was still outside. Finally, not only did he show up, but with one younger child in his arm and holding the hand of another. We were all so elated to see them all return safely. The next day at church, our leader expressed this joy and commended the young men for their bravery and willingness to sacrifice for the good of others.

Belief in God

Every year, unit leaders are encouraged to attend training at Wood Badge or Philmont Scout Ranch. I attended Wood Badge training during the summer of 1997, and it was held at Lassen Boy Scout Camp, eight miles south of Lassen Volcanic National Park in California. Generally, Wood Badge training is ten days long. To try and accommodate working adults, the training was broken up into two long weekends of four and three days. Participants are assigned to eight preassigned patrols of ten to twelve people. I must have been one of the first to sign up since I was assigned to the beaver patrol, which is always the first one organized.

Wood Badge training was what our troop was all about. At Wood Badge, all the trainees were playing the role of scouts and learning important concepts and skills. The training is focused on teaching scout leaders most of the general skills needed to assist scouts in becoming first class. It is also used to teach leaders how to effectively run the patrol method in scouting. Instead of a scout master, our patrol has a counselor. During our training sessions, if we had any questions about our tasks or objectives, the counselor would give the instructions to keep us on the right track. Usually near the end of the day after several training sessions, he would show up in our camp and review what we'd learned that day, and we would generate ideas of how we could use that to help scouting programs back home. The counselors and leaders of the camp were all volunteers and gave up ten days of their lives to provide us this training.

Wood Badge training is run like a BSA youth camp: reveille is at 7:00 a.m.; flags are at 7:45 a.m.; and between 7:00 and 7:45 a.m. is the time to get up, get ready, clean up camp, and head to flags. After flags and breakfast, classes and activities begin at 9:00 a.m. During the training, each patrol has several assignments such as providing the flag ceremony for the week, gathering wood for campfires, cleaning up the showers and bathrooms, and one assigned service project that needs to be executed during free time after the last training session but before dinner.

One of the more memorable activities was a hike with our patrol. We were told to pack some gear for an overnight camp and meet at a certain location. We thought this was just an exercise, but when we arrived at our rendezvous point, we were given a compass and a waypoint to find and told that when we reached our destination we would receive some supplies for the overnight camp. Since I'd thought this would be just an exercise, I hadn't packed as many supplies as I should have. We were given some instructions about preparations, such as making sure our packs were 25% of our body weight.

We started on our hike, with two patrol members checking the bearing and two members verifying the distance. In earlier activities, we'd learned how to measure our paces to judge one hundred feet and how to travel along a bearing over long distances to find a location. Our hike was three miles and not along any roads. In some locations the ground cover was thick, making it hard to maintain a straight course. After an hour or so hiking through the brush, we ended up in a clearing where most of the trees had been cut down, leaving tree trunks, low-lying brush, and ground cover. We spread out to look for our supplies, and within a couple of minutes one of the patrol members spotted our gear fifty yards from where we'd ended up, which wasn't bad. The supplies included food, cooking gear, and a couple of tents. After setting up camp, we cooked dinner, ate, sat around a fire, and went to bed. We had to get up and hike back to camp before flags the next morning.

Because this training was conducted over the weekend, I wasn't able to attend church with my family. Attending church with my family was a tradition. I don't think I missed church more than a few times in ten years. I lamented not being able to attend with them, but I would attend church there at Camp Lassen. The schedule on Sunday was mostly the same as the other days except that two hours were set aside after lunch for church services. Everyone met together in the amphitheater on a hillside surrounded with evergreen pines and firs for a camp-wide service followed by organizational services. The church service was conducted by the training staff and lasted forty-five minutes. I could see a meadow to the south and the other mountains around the camp. As I sat on a bench looking at my surroundings and listening to the talks that had been prepared, I felt inspired and comforted. I don't remember exactly what was said, but I could tell that these men had a deep belief in God. It was very moving. I was glad to be at Camp Lassen that day.

Respect for Life

Running the American River in a canoe from the Nimbus Dam to Watt Avenue was an activity we did on a yearly basis. The American River comes out of the Sierra Nevada Mountain foothills and is one of the cleanest I've seen in California. Along the river from the Folsom Dam all the way into Sacramento is a parkway along which deer, peacocks, turkeys, and almost any other kind of urban wildlife can be seen. Very little of the city is visible other than the occasional bridge or house along the bank. This provides a relaxing atmosphere for canoeing, gliding with the current through an environment similar to a nature preserve.

There is also enough white water to make this an optimum section for a scout troop to run. There are some areas of concern with sweepers and strainers. A sweeper is a tree that has fallen down over the river and has branches extending into the water. This is very dangerous because it can trap a canoe or person. A strainer is a tree or sapling that would usually be on dry land, but is under high water. These can trap canoes also. For these reasons it's important that the lead canoe has someone who can read the river and convey a safe route to avoid hazards like these.

When we ran the river in 2004, I had one experience that was quite memorable. The San Juan rapids are the most challenging part of the river, but they were also a popular spot to have lunch. They're not big as rapids go, but there is a good flow of water, and they can easily lift the front of a canoe by three feet. The river is just a few feet deep before the rapids, but drops to twenty or thirty feet deep after the rapids. Some people would play in the rapids while others would sit on the bank and eat. We would haul our boats back up the river and rerun the rapids sometimes because they were so extreme. Occasionally, we would jump in the river above the rapids and float through them with our life preservers on. After lunch, that's what I did. I put on my life jacket, walked up the river, jumped in, and swam toward the biggest part of the San Juan rapids for a little fun. I had seen many people do this before without incident.

Unfortunately, as I went over the rapid, the force of the current shot me down to the bottom of the river. I can remember looking up and barely being able to see the surface. I swam like crazy but didn't feel like I was making any progress due to the current. Seconds began to feel like minutes. I wasn't sure if I was stuck down in the hole or if I was going to make it out alive. I didn't know if the current was holding me down or pushing me around in the water, but the location of the dim light at the surface didn't seem to be moving. Eventually, I started to see the surface get closer and I popped up four hundred feet downstream.

By this time, I was pretty tired from trying to swim to the surface, but I still had to swim to shore. I continued fighting the fast-paced current of the river. Luckily I remembered some of my Boy Scout high adventure training and rolled over onto my back. I faced my body upriver with a slight angle toward shore that allowed the current to push me, and I backstroked a little until the water was shallow enough to stand up. This is a ferrying technique.

This experience has been a source of some deep reflection many times over the years, and every time I think of it, I'm grateful to be alive. I could have hit a rock while under the water, been knocked out or broken a bone, or been prevented from swimming to safety. This experience wasn't an enjoyable one, but it's a treasure to me because it caused me to value the life I have.

Members of Troop 248 running the San Juan rapids on the American River.

Honoring Country and Flag

In 2007, our scout camp was planned at Camp John Mensinger, a Boy Scout camp north of Yosemite National Park surrounded by large granite rock structures. This camp was significant because of a special campfire to celebrate one hundred years of Scouting. Lord Baden-Powell started the Boy Scouts in England on July 25, 1907. A special campfire was planned for July 25 to honor this, including a flag retirement ceremony.

The campfire area sat on a small cliff facing west over a little ravine with a side hill to the north and south. Along the cliff's edge was a handrail to keep people from falling off. The sunset from the campfire area was awesome. The sky was blue, stars came out, and we were sitting among tall evergreen trees while a slight, warm breeze blew. It was the perfect atmosphere for enjoying the program. We had a regular campfire with skits, songs, and stories. At the end was the flag retirement ceremony. One of the adult staff talked about a tradition he had for flag retirement ceremonies to collect a sample of the ashes after the fire had cooled and use it for the next ceremony. He took out a container of ashes, poured them into the fire, and recited a history of all the flags that had been retired and were part of those ashes. He then recounted where all the flags had come from that were going to be retired that night. In the morning, anyone who wanted to come by the campfire pit and get a sample of ashes was welcome to do so. I stopped by and collected a sample for myself and have tried to carry on this tradition.

The junior leaders retired twelve flags that night, one of which was a flag that had flown over the California state capitol. Four color guards were assigned to each flag. They would march toward the campfire ring with the folded flag, and then each guard would take a corner of the flag and stretch it out for display. The flag was then centered and lowered over the fire. When the center was mostly burned, the corners of the flag were folded back toward the center of the fire to ensure the entire flag was consumed. This procedure was repeated until all of the flags were retired. Generally weekly scout meetings start with the recitation of the Scout Oath, which begins, "On my honor I will do my best/To do my duty to God and my country…" Flag retirement ceremonies instill in a person what these concepts mean and how important they are for individuals and society to honor God and country.

A flag retirement ceremony is a reverent event, and every time I attend one I get a knot in my throat from the emotion. This event was even more special to me because it was the last Boy Scout camp I attended in California. We had already moved to Utah; my son and I had returned to California so he would be able to attend summer camp. I wanted to fulfill my last responsibility as a scout leader in that stake. When we had first moved to California and I was called to be a unit leader, I attended every week-long summer camp. I had made so many good friends and I hated to see all that come to an end.

Team Building

Over the years, I have planned more than a dozen backpack trips for scouts into the Uinta Wilderness in Utah. One area of particular interest is Red Castle. I have often planned back-packing trips to the northern slope. We would hike in from a place called China Meadows and continue past Lower Red Castle Lake. Depending on where you camp, this hike can be about eleven miles. Lower Red Castle Lake is at an elevation of eleven thousand feet and has many fir trees. Most of the ground is covered with grass, wildflowers, and small bushes. The contrast of the red mountains, dirt, and rocks with the blue sky, white clouds, and green foliage is inspiring.

On one of these backpack trips into the wilderness, I witnessed a great example of scouts demonstrating helpfulness, compassion, and sacrifice. We had planned and carried out a couple of preparatory hikes to allow us, the leaders, to evaluate each scout's skill level and physical capability before the stress of the actual hike. Unfortunately, for this trip we had a scout who hadn't been evaluated beforehand. After a couple of miles up the trail, he started complaining about the difficulty. We still had eight miles to go, so I got a little nervous.

Backpacking trips are demanding and strenuous; they require hard work and determination, and are a definite struggle for those who don't get regular exercise. Since scouts need to carry all of their necessities, including a tent, a sleeping bag, clothes, food, cooking implements, and other commodities, their backpacks get quite heavy and cumbersome. A good backpack shouldn't be more than 25% of a scout's body weight, as I mentioned earlier, but that's still plenty. When you're carrying a backpack, hiking miles and miles a day in the hot summer sun, and increasing and decreasing thousands of feet in elevation, it's difficult to maintain a happy and positive attitude. In fact, it can often be difficult to think about anything but the pain and suffering one feels while hiking along the trail.

This young man on the way to Red Castle was physically capable, but his mind limited what he thought he could do. A good way to determine if a young man is not physically capable while exercising is to see if he can speak; if he can, he is not overexerting himself. This young man was sweating and working hard, but he was definitely able to speak.

After a couple more miles with many complaints from this young man, some of the other boys started volunteering to carry his pack as well as their own. Several boys assisted in this effort, too. After a couple more miles, I think this young man felt that if the other boys could carry two packs and hike without complaining, so could he. We didn't hear as many complaints from him after that.

This trip showed me that in a world of selfish interests, young men can make choices to help and support friends in need. I also saw a young man grow and mature. I have known some young men who would have preferred to play team sports rather than participate in scouting. Backpacking is a good example of why I think scouting can incorporate more desired characteristics. When a young man completes a difficult task by himself, he knows what he has accomplished. When a young man completes a team effort, he can't be sure of how much he contributed. In the end, the boy who accomplished the task by himself is much more thrilled and self-confident.

In a scouting environment, there are leaders and friends nearby for encouragement, but the effort is all individual. Backpacking provides an awesome opportunity to do a hard thing and have support from the troop while doing it. A boy is more willing to try other hard tasks if he has already successfully completed one. In the troop, many more of these opportunities exist.

Members of Troop 743 backpacking into the Red Castle basin

Friendliness

Southern Utah holds a special place in my memories. When I was seven years old, our family moved to Utah, and my dad would take us on vacations to southern Utah to many of the state parks. My father was born in Escalante, Utah, and much of my family is from that area. My dad and his brothers loved to hunt deer, and were familiar with many places to do so in central and southern Utah. On some of our vacations, we would stop at a trading post and a rock shop to buy souvenirs. Southern Utah has some unique landscape with lots of red sandstone rock structures, cliffs from the Colorado Plateau, and canyons carved out by the flowing rivers. The red sandstone is a soft type of rock that can be etched with other rocks, metal, and wood. From the Island in the Sky, you can see the endless ravines created by the Green and Colorado Rivers for probably one hundred miles in many directions. You can see the white-capped La Sal Mountains to the southeast and Dead Horse Point, the confluence of the Colorado and Green Rivers.

All around Moab are red sandstone cliffs. When it snows in the winter, the contrast between the red and white is beautiful. When the sun goes down on clear summer evenings, the red sunlight reflects off cirrus clouds, and the cliffs seem almost like they are on fire. Due to the heat of the summer, though, the best time to visit this area of Utah is late spring or late fall. In and around Moab are dozens of trails of varying degrees of difficulty and terrain for hiking and mountain biking. Whenever I take a group of scouts to Moab for mountain biking, I like to take them to the Slickrock Practice Loop, which is made up of miles of rolling hills of red sandstone. Riding a bike on sandstone is like riding on sandpaper because your tires grip like crazy, but you can ride up steep rock structures if you have enough strength in your legs.

There are so many exciting trails to ride in Moab, and each is special for different reasons. Onion Creek is fun because the trails go through the stream a couple dozen times, and it's a challenge to get in front of one of your friends going through the creek so he gets all wet. Porcupine Rim is a test of strength and endurance. Slickrock is challenging because many of the routes are so difficult that it really tests your abilities. Every ride or hike has spectacular views.

The first time I rode the Slickrock Trail, I rode down a steep section of rock and flipped over the handlebars more than once. When you come down a steep grade and there is a crevasse changing the slope between the rocks' surfaces, that resistance change can cause you to flip. This causes a couple injuries. As I mentioned, the rock is like sandpaper, and you can imagine what it's like to fall on sandpaper. When you finally get used to this environment, riding on the rock is amazing, especially because your tires grip so well.

Riding in Moab can challenge one's strength, skill, and endurance. During one trip we had scheduled challenging and strenuous activities, and started the trip with practicing biking skills at Slickrock Trail. We had boys of all skill levels to whom we wanted to teach and practice biking skills to allow them to become more confident in their abilities.

On one ride we rode from the upper parking lot to an area called Gemini Bridges, ate lunch, and drove out to the lower parking lot. The total overall distance was twenty-one miles. According to the schedule, we were to go into Arches National Park and hike to Delicate Arch. When we arrived at the lower parking lot, the boys didn't want to get out of the car, so we drove around the park looking at interesting rock structures and the awesome landscape. In the morning, the boys were refreshed and agreed to do the hike to Delicate Arch.

Sometimes, individuals not used to riding bikes on long, rough roads get sore backsides because of the pounding of their backside against the seat. To elaborate a little about why people get sore backsides when they are not used to riding bikes: When riding bikes on trails and dirt roads, you usually ride over rocks, ledges, washboards, sticks, etc. and after many miles of these kinds of conditions, it's kind of hard on the backside. When I was riding my road bike in California, I would ride one hundred miles a week, and if I ever took a two- or three-month break from riding, I would need to get used to biking again. The first day back usually wouldn't be so bad, but the second day would be very bothersome sitting in the seat. You can imagine what it would be like after riding a mountain bike.

When we were hiking up to Delicate Arch, I could see that one of our boys was struggling and it wasn't due to sore feet or sore legs. We made it to the arch, took pictures, and started back down the trail when I heard this scout encourage a hiker on the way up. He said, "Keep on going, you're almost there. The hike is worth it!" He made similar comments to hikers all the way back down. Most kids would have complained in his situation rather than encourage others.

**Members of Troop 743 at Delicate Arch after hiking up
from the parking lot.**

Leadership

Leadership is a significant characteristic that I thought needs some elaboration, especially in the context of scouting. The scouting program is set up so that the youth are the leaders, not the adult volunteers. In the BSA, leadership assignments start at eleven years old. It is so important that leadership requirements are attached to rank advancement. For example, the Star rank advancement requires four months of leadership. Generally, the senior patrol leader is the overall leader of the troop, and he is supported by the assistant senior patrol leader. The troop is then divided up into patrols with a patrol leader and an assistant. The troop is divided into as many patrols as needed to make leading the troop easier to manage.

Once a week there is a patrol leaders' council, where the activities of the troop are discussed and managed, run by the senior patrol leader and attended by all the leaders in the troop and the Scoutmaster. Adult leaders attend these meeting, but only to offer suggestions to assist and ensure important topics are covered. After the meeting, the adults usually will counsel the senior patrol leader to offer ways to improve his leadership.

When a scout accepts a leadership position, there's not generally any formal training, although there are many classes available. What usually happens is that the scout is given a responsibility, and then is given the page in the Boy Scout handbook that describes what each position's responsibilities are. He is then requested to attend a junior leader training class, usually provided by the adult leadership. Afterward, they learn as they go or get help from the person who had that job previously.

Scouts also develop leadership skill when they select, plan, organize, and carry out Eagle service projects for nonprofit organizations, communities, federal or state parks, or specific individuals in need. These projects should be executed by as many scouts, friends, and family as the scout can recruit. Overall, the project should involve sixty-four hours of service, including the young man's planning and organizing. It is the young man's responsibility to lead all aspects of the project. One example that struck me was a young man who was participating in a baseball league who wanted to improve the park where he usually played.

He talked to the president of the league, who suggested building a dugout for the minor B field and offered to pay for the materials. The young man drew up some plans and presented them to the park superintendent for approval. Afterward, the young man went to a fence company to get a list of materials and to find out how much they would cost. The cost was given to the league so that funds could be acquired to pay for the fencing materials. The boy then scheduled times to have people whom he had recruited show up at the park to help build the dugouts. Scouts would drill holes, cement fence posts into place, stretch and fasten chain link fencing to the posts, and build and fix a roof to the new dugout. Finally, the young man got the approval for the completion of the project from the president of the baseball league and the park superintendent.

Let me share another favorite example of a time when a scout was faced with some significant peer pressure and leadership challenges. We were at a week-long summer camp at

Camp Loll near Grand Teton National Park. During the camp, our group elected to do a hike as an activity for the older boys, in part to test the young men's ability to follow and find a location with a map and compass. Our troop guide gave us the map and compass, and showed us the location on the map that we were going to have to find. We quickly reviewed the skills of orienting the map and turned the effort over to the young men. They oriented the map, found the direction to travel, and we were off. One group of boys was focused on checking our distance, and another group focused on our direction. We hiked for two miles, and as we gained elevation, the trees started to thin out. Eventually we were able to identify landmarks on the map and could tell we were heading in the right direction. We eventually found the trail that would lead to our destination peak.

It was in the Grand Teton range, four to five miles from Camp Loll. It wasn't one of the more famous peaks, but it was memorable just the same. There were creeks; ponds; open, green, flower-filled fields; patches of fir and pine trees; and some occasional wildlife. We could see for sixty to eighty miles in all directions. It was spectacular.

On the way back, the lower elevation brought back the heavier forestation and a loss of landmarks. The boys opened the map and roughly located our position on the map. We hiked for a mile or more, but none of the landscape seemed familiar. We stopped to reevaluate our direction, but at this point some of the boys became concerned that we were lost and started to suggest their own plans. One wanted to follow the ravine, another suggested hiking up the hillside to see if we could view a familiar structure, but one of the patrol leaders said that we were okay and needed to trust our process to find the camp. The rest of the boys felt this patrol leader's confidence and followed him farther down the hill. Within one quarter of a mile we could see the camp almost right in front of us! We ended up arriving in camp two hundred yards west of where we had left. It turned out our troop guide had been on the hike at least once a week all summer long and knew the way back to camp. He had wanted to test the boys' abilities to use a map and compass.

Because of the extensive leadership opportunities afforded by the Boy Scouts and the experiences that come with them, young men tend to develop skills of goal setting, organization, preparation, public speaking, better communication, and good decision making. Can you imagine how successful a young man would be with these leadership skills?

Members of Troop 743 on hike through the wilderness

Developing Good Decision Making

Many times I have pondered what I would help my kids develop if I wanted them to have one trait or skill to help them be successful and self-sufficient. I have concluded it would be best to train them to make good decisions. This is one awesome benefit I like about the Boy Scouts: It provides one of the best environments for teaching a boy to make good decisions.

I've heard it said that a person can learn four different ways: First, one can learn from another person's knowledge. Second, one can learn from the example of another person. Third, one can learn from reading. Fourth, one can learn from one's mistakes. This last method seems better to me because the consequences of a bad decision are a powerful reminder. One of the best ways to become a great decision maker is in an environment where the consequences are immediate but not severe. Suppose a troop goes winter camping and a boy decides to wear tennis shoes instead of snow boots. The consequence is that the boy gets cold feet almost immediately. He made a choice and it has an immediate but mild consequence. When the consequences are immediate, the learning from a decision is accelerated. On a campout, the decision-making process and dealing with its aftermath can happen dozens of times a day. No environment I've dealt with can even come close to scouting at developing great decision making.

I believe it is a disservice when parents rescue their children from the consequences of poor choices. How will a youth learn to make better decisions if parents seek to remove the consequences of his decision? Where will the encouragement to make better choices come from? How will a child grow and mature if he doesn't see life as it really is? I have noticed that many parents don't have many expectations for their kids, like doing chores around the house or requiring a specific level of achievement at school. Some parents have no issue buying their kids the latest gadgets, fashions, or transportation. Parents should meet their child's needs, not wants.

Members of Troop 743 during the Klondike Derby standing on top of the Igloo that they just slept in

Rafting the Green River

In July 1979, I was a member of the Boy Scouts. My troop rafted the Green River in Utah from just below the Flaming Gorge Dam to the city of Green River. The river only has a couple of entry points along that stretch and most of them are close to the city because the river has cut a canyon in the soil and rock, making walls two hundred feet high and very steep. They are almost unclimbable for inexperienced youths. The Green River runs through dry and rocky ground that limits the vegetation and wildlife. The water is not very clear, and after just one day on the river we felt like we were covered in a film of dirt.

On the second day of the trip, some of my friends and I were hiking and found a small stream. We spent an hour digging a pool that it would feed into so we could take a bath the next morning. We couldn't bathe in the river because the river water is what had made us dirty in the first place. When we arrived at the pool for our baths, we found that the water was stirred up with silt and a layer of soap. We didn't get our baths that day.

For this trip we had five or six eight-man rafts and one large equipment supply raft. The supply raft was narrow and long with a motor so it could maneuver around and miss any problems. We also had a large raft rowed by a single man who sat in a framework attached to it. In the eight-man rafts, everyone was required to wear a life jacket and everyone had a paddle to help steer. Each eight-man raft had a leader who would instruct the others what to do.

Most of us scouts on this trip had little rafting or canoeing experience. On the first day of the trip, the water was mostly calm except for one hole that we hit near the end of the day. Since we were young, inexperienced, and new to white-water rafting, we paddled to the hole. I think our raft was the first to hit the hole and we had no clue what would happen; we thought the raft would ride right through it. Instead, the raft dropped into the hole, the backflow folded the raft in half, and everyone got tossed into the water except me. I became concerned for the safety of my friends and my younger brother. Luckily, all but three of the kids were picked up by other rafts. I was stuck in the hole and couldn't get the boat out, so I tried different things to get unstuck and in doing so fell in anyway. This gave the raft enough momentum to get out of the hole, and when I surfaced, I spotted the raft, swam to it, and climbed in. I was able to get to my three remaining friends and pull them in. That was an exciting end to day one!

On the second day, the leader of the expedition was in our eight-man raft. We were floating down a calm section and every boat was engaged in a fun water fight when suddenly the leader said we had to paddle over toward a rock sticking up out of the water. It turned out that section of the river was known as "The Needles" and was full of larger boulders that generated miniature waterfalls between them. Since the other boats weren't paying attention, they missed that challenge. When we approached one waterfall, the front of the raft hit one of the boulders. One of the kids sitting in the front fell forward, hit his head, and fell into the water. I looked at the waterfall and thought we were going to flip the raft for sure. Somehow we made it through and were able to pick up the kid who'd fallen in. Thankfully, his head injury was minor and didn't even cause any bleeding.

This trip happened during the first or last week of July, both of which are usually celebrated with fireworks. During the trip, one of the river guides who had brought some fireworks started lighting them about dusk. One of them was a bottle rocket which had poor propulsion and direction, and it landed on the other side of the river. Its black powder was still burning when it landed, which started a fire. Because of the darkness and the swift current, we couldn't risk crossing the river. Luckily, the fire went out after ten minutes.

On the last day, the river was flowing fast and in some areas had standing waves. It was like riding a roller coaster. Some of the youths jumped out of the rafts altogether to float the rapids with their life jackets. It wasn't long before we made it to Green River, packed up, took showers, and headed for home. What I remember best about this trip was that I unexpectedly made some great friends. It also taught me that even adults can struggle with making good decisions and can learn from their mistakes. We never stop learning.

Grover Hot Springs

As far as winter camps go, Grover Hot Springs is a winner. It's a California State Park near South Lake Tahoe and west of Markleeville that allows camping all year round. It's nestled on an east slope of the Sierra Nevada Mountains so it doesn't get a lot of snow in the wintertime, but there is enough to enjoy most winter activities. Near the state park is a hot spring that's been developed into an outdoor facility with two swimming pools. One has a cooler temperature and is equipped with a diving board, while the other is 105°F and is filled with a mixture of the water from the hot springs and cooler water. It has become a tradition to see if anyone would be brave enough to get out of the pools, lie down in the snow, and make snow angels. I've only witnessed two conditions there: wet and cold, or clear and very cold. The pools stay open late into the evening, so we could play in the snow and get warm in the springs before bed. It's relaxing to sit in the warm pool in the wintertime and look out at the snow-covered trees and mountains.

Generally, to stay warm at night for winter camp, it's helpful to have several feet of snow to build a shelter. At Grover Hot Springs, we have never been able to build an igloo or snow cave due to the lack of snow. The first year we went, there was hardly any snow at all. We arrived near dark, so we set up tents for some people and others slept in the back of trucks. I don't remember getting any sleep because it was so cold. Fortunately, that was the only time we went when there wasn't at least a few inches of snow on the ground. The most

popular shelter we have used at this location was developed
by a member of the Okpik HAT by placing a large tarp over a
rope tied between two trees. The ends were blocked up with
snow or another tarp. This shelter is somewhat better than a
tent, as it's large and can be built quickly. Since the ground can
be conditioned before the tarp is put on, a fairly level sleeping
surface can be achieved and a cold sink can be incorporated.
We had as many as twenty people in one of these kinds of
shelters.

To the south of the campground is an evergreen-forested
hill with clearings that is a great place for winter festivities.
Snowball fights and sleigh riding take up most of the free
time. To the west of Grover Hot Springs is a great place to
snowshoe along the stream that comes out of the mountain.
Since the temperatures are mostly below freezing, layers of
ice cover the slow-moving water. Some ice dams form and
back up the water to make a little pool, which eventually flows
over the obstruction. It is beautiful.

Winter camp significantly increases the number of decisions young men need to make, which increases their decision-making skills.

Members of Troop 248 in the pool at Grover Hot Springs

Point Reyes Backpacking

Backpacking in Point Reyes National Seashore is always a treasure, especially staying at Coast Camp on the northwestern boundary. We usually park on the east side of the coastal range and hike along the ridges that run from the backbone to the coast. Coast Camp is a few hundred feet from the ocean on the other side of a hill fifty feet high, nestled between a couple of ridges protecting it from the full force of the coastal winds. To get to the beach, we would need to walk only two hundred feet to the north and west. Coast Camp is mostly open ground, and the soil is covered by grasses, other low-profile ground cover, and small bushes. At night, when camp starts to settle down, we could see dozens of red, beady eyes looking out from the brush. If no one is at the camp, these red-and-beady-eyed creatures, raccoons, come out to pillage the camp for food. That's why it's a good idea to make sure any food is secure in a container that the raccoons can't open or eat their way through. The campground provides metal storage containers for each campsite, but many kids forget and leave something out in a backpack or something. This usually means that in the morning there is a hole chewed through the fabric of the backpack and the food is gone.

There are many things to do at Coast Camp. A favorite activity is to find creatures in the tide pools when the tide goes out. I have always loved finding crabs, starfish, sea snails, and such. One time we were having a campfire on the beach shortly after the tide went out. Afterward, I was walking along the beach on my way back to camp and everywhere I stepped my footprints glowed a pale neon green. It turned out to be unicellular algae that glows when it is disturbed. It was interesting to see a glowing green path of footprints down the beach.

Like with all high-adventure activities—backpacking, river running, and winter camping—the troop provided high-adventure training (HAT) before the trip. Part of the backpack training is discussing keeping your pack as light as possible, and good and bad food choices. I've mentioned before how the best weight ratio for a pack is one-fourth of a scout's body weight. For this reason, it's better not to carry too much liquid because of increased weight; it's more practical and safer to use a water filter. Also, soda is bad due to some of its ingredients that get into the blood and prevent oxygen absorption. Well, on one trip to Point Reyes, a scout brought a six-pack of Mountain Dew, which weighs five pounds. For a boy who weighs eighty pounds, the target pack weight is twenty pounds or less, so this was unnecessary. After the first day of backpacking, he was giving the soda away to the other scouts before dinner.

On the northwest boundary of the beach is a lighthouse available to tour Thursday through Monday. The Point Reyes Lighthouse is only thirty-five feet tall due to its location on a hill. It was built in 1870 after the area was named the second foggiest in North America and was manned up to 1975, after which an automated light was installed and ownership was turned over to the National Park Service. There are three structures painted white with red roofs. The lighthouse uses a six-thousand-pound Fresnel lens that can be seen by ships from up to twenty-four miles away. This doubled the distance of most lighthouses that used mirrors. There is a beautiful beach just down from the lighthouse, but it is has a dangerous undertow. If you're the kind of person who loves to watch large waves crash, this is the place for you.

On our troop's first backpacking trip through Point Reyes, the hiking group was spread out and the leaders weren't sure if all the scouts had taken the right forks in the trail. The Point Reyes wilderness has an east and west area divided by a small mountain that's part of the coastal range and several trails on each side that intersect with a trail that runs along the north and south. Due to this trail configuration, it was difficult to know if the scouts had taken the right trail from the ridge down to the coast or on the way back home to the parking lot. We decided to use walkie-talkies from then on.

River Running: The Sacramento River

Shortly after George Gettys and I attended the HAT training "Paddle Sports," our troop decided to plan a trip to run the Sacramento River from Redding, CA, to Red Bluff. In an effort to reduce the boats the troop would need to rent, George decided to buy a kayak, and I bought a canoe. This was a fun trip that included camping two nights at Anderson Park and at Bend Campground. The flow of the river just below the Sundial Bridge can be as fast as 40,000 cubic feet per second, but during the summer months it's usually less than 20,000. This results in speeds from four to ten miles per hour depending on the cross-section of the river. The water comes out of Shasta Dam and can be very cold even in the hottest summer months. The banks of the river are lined with oaks, elms, and cottonwood trees, and a variety of bushes. The total distance was fifty-six miles, but it was broken up into three sections. The first section was from Redding to Anderson, twenty-two miles, followed by twenty-six miles from Anderson to Bend RV Campground. The last leg was from Bend to Red Bluff and was only eight miles, most of which was flat and slow.

We launched the canoes and kayaks at Turtle Bay Exploration Park by Sundial Bridge in Redding. The average width of the river is probably three to four hundred feet. For this trip, we had a couple who came along to help shuttle the cars and cook the food. This meant all we had to be concerned with was getting the boys safely down the river, but that is not always the easiest thing to do. On the east side of the first stretch of the river is an inlet water source that is bathtub warm with a rope swing thirty feet above it tied to the branch of a nearby oak tree. If you climbed up the trunk of the tree, you could swing out over the water and get fifteen feet of additional air. A couple of the kids had gymnastics backgrounds and tried to do flips while swinging out. We stopped for an hour to let anyone use the swing or have fun. It was a nice location to play in the water, relax, eat, and take pictures.

Anderson has a nice park along the river where the grass runs right up to the water, and we were able to pull our crafts up onto the lawn. Some of us set up tents by the water and boats, while others slept under the stars. During the summer, Anderson Park has concerts that are fun to attend. Their facilities include covered picnic tables, huge six-foot-by-twelve-foot barbeque grills, and tennis courts. Since we had chefs travelling with us, we ate barbeque steak that night and had enough time to go into town to see a movie. We ended up seeing *Mr. and Mrs. Smith*.

The second day of the trip was probably the most challenging because of the Chinese Rapids. Eddies form at confluences and around obstructions in the water, and while they are not too dangerous, the adverse directions of the currents can easily flip a canoe. Young, unprepared boys can easily be flipped out of their crafts, or the canoe can roll over. Grabbing a canoe's side rail and leaning is the easiest way to flip it. Part of Paddle Sport training was on how to stabilize a canoe in adverse situations: Put your paddle in the water with the wide section in the direction of the undesired movement and apply pressure against the paddle that opposes that movement.

In this area of the river were many fifteen-foot wide whirl-pools with two-foot-deep swells. A friend of mine was caught in one and had to be rescued by someone on shore with a rope. My canoe had two young men, including my son Adam and me, and we hit one of the whirlpools. It immediately rotated the canoe at a right angle, but we still had forward momentum, so everyone was thrown into the water. Most of our group was ahead of us so the boys were rescued by some of the other canoers. I collected ours and we were on our way again. That was an exciting day!

Our second overnight stay was at Bend RV Campground. The river was more narrow, causing the flow of water to increase, and the bank is steeper and recessed from an out-cropping of rocks. With the steeper bank, the water in the pull-out area for the crafts is deep with a nonvisible bottom. This condition made the depth of the water difficult to determine before climbing out of the boat. Several people thought the water was shallower than it was and almost fell into waist-deep water. Eventually, we all got settled at the campground and most of the boys and adults made their way to the country store to buy ice cream sandwiches, candy bars, or soda pop.

The last leg of the trip, from Bend to Red Bluff, started with four miles of swift water and finished with four miles of slow water. I think it required more work to paddle the last four miles than all the other miles of the journey. Halfway through these last four miles was another tree swing, with a platform on a second tree that helped some of the boys get several more feet above the water when they let go of the rope. The water temperature was much colder here, though. After some fun and a little more paddling, it was time to load up and head home. It was a good end to a great trip.

Members of Troop 248 near Sundial bridge at the start of the Sacramento River trip

Snowshoeing to Peter Grubb Hut

The winter clothing system taught in Okpik keeps people warm because it keeps moisture away from the body. When water changes from a liquid to a vapor, it removes heat (energy) from its surroundings, and if the water is against one's skin, it takes heat from one's body. Water is always changing states from a solid to a liquid or from a liquid to a vapor. The process increases as the temperature increases. This means that any clothing damp with water will get colder than the air temperature. Okpik training teaches a three-layer clothing system: a wick layer, an insulating layer, and then a shell layer. The wick layer's job is to pull moisture away from the body; thermal underwear is the most common material used for this layer. If you're buying thermal underwear, make sure it isn't made of cotton. Cotton traps moisture rather than conducting it away. The insulating layer also needs to be able to wick moisture away but also provide insulation. This layer is usually a synthetic fleece. Shell layers can be as thin as a wind breaker; the main requirements of the shell layer are that it be waterproof, windproof, and breathable. It should be made of wool or synthetic material which prevents it from absorbing moisture. To control body temperature, make adjustments to each clothing layer, such as unzipping the shell layer or taking off the insulation layer. The objective is to stay comfortable, but not too hot. If you get hot, your body perspires and your clothes dampen. Even if the right clothing dries out faster, it's better not to need to dry it out in the first place. All this came in handy whenever we went snowshoeing at Peter Grubb Hut.

Peter Grubb Hut and the Castle Peaks area is fun for scout activities during both winter and summer. It is located just off Interstate 80 in the Sierra Nevada Mountains, three miles north of the Boreal Ski Resort. During the wintertime, the area is covered with evergreen trees and deep snow. The hike to get to Peter Grubb Hut starts north of the freeway, inclining up a hillside for half a mile, then along a small canyon for two miles. The incline then increases on top of a ridgeline and flattens out until it reaches the hut. From a short distance to the west, the view looks down a hillside but extends for nearly hundreds of miles to the south and west. The Sierras have a slow, gradual elevation on the west, from Sacramento to Donner's Summit. At Donner's Summit the elevation is more than 7,000 feet; the hut is more than 500 to 1,000 feet above that.

The hut is Sierra Club property and is available year round with no reservation or scheduling programs. It is a two-story building that can hold forty people, with the lower level made of cinder block and the upstairs loft being the A-frame structure of the roof. In the basement is a kitchen area with counters, tables, and chairs. There is no running water, but solar panels charge a battery pack to run the lights at night. Also, downstairs is a wood stove with a room full of wood that has been collected during the summer. Volunteers in the summer gather, cut, split, and deposit the wood in the cabin for winter use. During the winter the snow is usually ten feet deep, requiring visitors to enter the hut from the loft. The outhouse is located twenty to thirty feet away and is built on a pedestal nine to ten feet high so it can be used in winter. You can imagine what this looks like in the summer.

One of our first experiences going to Peter Grubb Hut was not successful. We started the trip on a Friday after the boys had come home from school; with the early winter sunsets and distance of travel, we arrived at the Boreal parking lot at six o'clock p.m. It was a clear night and cold. The temperature felt like it must have been in the single digits. There was no moon but enough light that we could somewhat see where we were going. After hiking for thirty minutes, I had to stop and take off my coat because I was so hot. We had one scout who had not participated in the training that we had provided and used galoshes for winter boots, which have no thermal insulation. At the end of the hike, his feet had some frost nip, but we helped him warm up and he was okay. We finally made it to the top of the ridge and hiked to where we thought the hut was, but couldn't find it. We hiked around for another thirty minutes but still couldn't find it, and had to hike back down the hill and drive home. Since we never made it to the hut, no one had dinner until we got home around midnight. We learned as leaders how critical it is that all boys participate in the cold weather awareness training.

We have been to Peter Grubb Hut many times and have enjoyed many entertaining activities there. One year, the scouts dug out a snow cave from the side of a snowbank on the side of the hill. This cave was much warmer than sleeping outside in a tent. The next day was clear and sunny, so the kids spent most of the morning sleigh riding and having snowball fights. After a couple of hours, one of the boys came running because one of the other scouts had fallen down a hole. He said they had been running after each other when the other boy just dropped out of sight. I ran to the scene and lay down on the snow to try and get him out, but there was a three- to four-foot gap between our hands. I was concerned about digging around the top of the hole for fear of the snow collapsing in on top of him or covering him with debris while digging. We started digging two feet away from the hole. After we had dug down five feet, we tried to compact and dig out the snow between the hole we had dug and the hole into which the scout had fallen. I reached down from there and was able to pull him up and out.

It turned out that the hole had been created by a hidden stream of water that was still running and had eroded the snow from underneath. The scout had stood on a rock inside the hole to keep from falling into the water. This experience showed the importance of taking the time to evaluate the consequence of choices before they're made and to decide on a course of action that provides the best outcome.

Troop 248 in front of the Peter Grubb Hut near Castle Peak in the Sierras. The snow is about 10' deep so entrance is from the second story loft.

Winter Camping

The BSA provides three High Adventure Team (HAT) training courses to aid Boy Scout leaders with the information and skills required to conduct high-adventure activities. They are Paddle Sports, Backpackers Awareness, and Okpik (cold weather awareness). These courses are offered to help train adult leaders so they can provide their troops with high-adventure activities and maintain a higher level of success and safety. HAT courses have allowed me many wonderful experiences both in scouting and personally. They deliver practical knowledge that I have found useful in everyday life, have helped me enjoy winter camping much more, and in at least one instance have probably saved my life. In the BSA, high-adventure activities are for the older, more experienced, and capable scouts because of the assimilation of characteristics above and beyond the base program. A scout can always learn good decision making, determination, the value of hard work, and maturity, but HAT activities take this to the next level.

I have learned from HAT how important it is to be well trained before planning and carrying out high-adventure activities. In addition, I have learned how and what clothing to wear to stay warm in cold weather conditions. It has also shown me that many clothing suppliers have no idea what kind of material should be used in cold weather clothing. I have learned how to plan, organize, train, and evaluate scouts.

Looking back, I can see that HAT training has significantly improved my ability as a scout leader to provide successful and safe high-adventure activities.

Okpik is the cold weather awareness training provided by HAT, named after a snow owl. Winter camping has become one of my favorite outdoor adventures, mainly because I learned how to do it comfortably. I had tried winter camping a few times before going through Okpik as a scout leader and was not successful. Okpik training was given in two sections: an in-class section and an outdoor section. The training covered trip planning, equipment use, shelters, clothing, safety, reading the landscape (avalanche precautions), food needs, and first aid. My outdoor session for the course was held at Sugar Pine State Park on the west shore of Lake Tahoe. The objectives were to build a snow shelter large enough for my group and to sleep in it overnight. Our choices for a shelter were a snow cave and an igloo, but I had tried building snow caves before on some earlier camps and wasn't too impressed, so we decided to build an igloo. This was my first attempt at that.

A good snow shelter accomplishes three goals: protection from the elements such as the rain, snow, and wind; provision of some insulation from the cold temperatures; and a location for the cold air to go like a cold sink. A cold sink is a drop near the entrance to the igloo a couple of feet deep that extends out beyond the wall. It allows the cold air to sink so the warm air can rise for the people inside. Many types of snow shelters exist, but the best ones have an encasement of snow with a cold sink. As you can imagine, tents and tarp-like structures only address one of the three factors, so they are not good winter shelters. When it comes to snow-encased shelters, there are many sizes and types depending on how many people need shelter and how much time you have to build.

Snow caves can hold a large number of people, but depending on the conditions while digging out the hole, you can run into rocks and trees that reduce the area or the flatness of the sleeping space. Snow caves also take a long time to construct. Igloos, on the other hand, can hold a lot of people, have level floors, and have more room for standing. They might be difficult to build if the snow is dry and powdery, but they can be constructed faster and stronger when the conditions are right. If the snow is powdery, the ice blocks used for building materials will break apart and won't stick to the other blocks very well. Having an optimal temperature is also important; if the temperature isn't within an acceptable range, the blocks won't stick to each other. Igloos have a large, open interior, allowing for cooking and entertainment.

Igloos are built by first preparing an area on which to build. It's helpful if the snow is at least three to four feet deep; this allows enough depth to dig a cold sink. It's better if the snow can be even deeper so you can cut out a layer of blocks from inside the igloo, instantly providing two feet of wall height. It's a good idea to use a rope that is half the diameter of the igloo base. The end of the rope is tied to a stick, buried in the snow, and used to measure where the walls go and their curvature as they grow. You will need an area or two to use as a quarry for ice blocks close to the igloo, but not right next to it. You don't want to have to carry the blocks too far and you will be passing them over the wall to the builder on the inside.

Blocks for an igloo are made by using a ridged piece of plastic with a handle that is pushed into the snow to cut the width and length of the block. To start the quarry for the ice blocks, you will need to dig a four-square-foot pit to the depth you want the blocks to be. (I would recommend one square foot by two feet long.) The larger the block, the faster the build, of course, but if the blocks are too big your back will be killing you by the time you're done. The first few blocks won't be the full one foot in height because they'll be establishing the base. The walls are created by placing blocks around the base and slowly sloping up from one block to the next. With the blocks sloping up, the block being inserted exerts pressure on the block next to it and the block below it. This process continues around the circumference and upward until the igloo is enclosed. During the building process, the builder will need to trim the blocks with a knife for the best fit.

In an igloo, the temperature never gets below 40°F because it is fully enclosed in snow; to keep the people inside warm, the design incorporates a cold sink and relies on body heat. Since ice and snow are 32°F at their warmest, the inside surface of the igloo cannot go below freezing, but people can still stay quite warm. If the temperature inside the igloo gets above freezing, care must be taken to ensure the inside of the igloo is smooth. Otherwise water from the melting snow will find a protrusion and drip on you, which is very unpleasant. The igloo we built at Okpik had a thirteen-foot-wide base and a six-foot-high ceiling. It took four adults three and a half hours to build and was big enough to hold five or six of us. For our first igloo, this was a pretty fast time, according to one of the instructors.

Usually in the morning after sleeping inside an igloo, we see how many people we can get on top of it before it collapses. We managed to get eleven people on top of this one. For all the igloos we have built over the years, we have never been able to collapse them the next morning, unless it was compromised by rain or scouts. The year before, some of the scouts started to destroy the igloo by cutting through the walls. Even with this structural compromise, more than eleven individuals had to jump up and down on top of the igloo before it broke.

Do you know how to stay warm at night while sleeping in winter conditions? It's easy if you pay attention to a few simple concepts. First, insulate your body from the ground by using an added layer of something like cardboard. Foam and air mattresses don't do a very good job since there is usually an area where your body completely condenses the material and comes into contact with the ground. Putting a layer of cardboard under the foam or air mattress will prevent this. Second, make sure to sleep in a zero-degree sleeping bag. To improve the warmth, a sleeping bag liner made of fleece does a good job. Third, make sure to wear clean, dry clothes to bed; if any of your clothes are wet, the vaporization process will reduce body temperature. Fourth, wear an insulated hat, like a fleece hat. Sixty percent of your body heat is lost through your head. Fifth, get all body parts warm before going to bed. Try sitting by the fire for a little while. Sixth, eat a warm meal with a large volume of warm fluids. Following these steps will ensure a warm night's sleep.

For the equipment part of the Okpik training, two men named Erik and Carl from Adventure Sports provided cloth-ing, knowledge, and demonstrations. To show how synthetic clothing absorbs less water and dries out faster than cotton, they had us wear a wet cotton shirt and a wet synthetic shirt during the training to see which one was driest at the end. The synthetic shirt felt dry within an hour, while the cotton shirt still felt damp after three.

Our troop provided winter camp training before engaging in winter camp activities. It focused on clothing, nutrition, staying hydrated, and staying warm. It would take two to three sessions before the boys would remember most of the information. Our troop occasionally had young men who weren't that interested in scouting but wanted to go to the camp. One year a boy who didn't get the training went on a snowshoe hike. He didn't wear the proper gear and his feet were frost nipped in two hours. This was the worst incident I encountered in twenty years, but fortunately nothing was lost. But for this reason, it is critical to ensure every boy receive winter camp training, including recognizing signs of frost bite and hypothermia. Hypothermia is when the core temperature of the body drops below 95°F. Scout leaders and scouts should pay close attention to the signs of hypothermia in the others around him, since a scout suffering from hypothermia may not be aware of his condition. One of the first signs is shivering followed by mental confusion. If a scout is experiencing hypothermia, he should be warmed using the following method: take off any wet clothes and put on dry clothes, get him into a warm environment if possible, and get him to drink warm fluids.

During the training, the question was posed, "If your foot had frostbite and you had no way to call for help and eight miles to hike to help, what should you do?" The answer was you hike even with the frostbitten foot. If you don't hike out, you won't make it. If you hike out with the frostbitten foot, you will make it out, even though you will probably lose the foot.

Participation in wintertime activities might require someone with the ability to read the landscape to avoid avalanches, though avalanches are rare. I don't mean to downplay the danger of an avalanche because they are dangerous, and without trained personnel and equipment they can be deadly. Of all the winter camps I've been on, none of them had avalanche danger. If someone is buried in an avalanche, you have only fifteen minutes to get that person out before his chances of survival diminish. Without a beacon, finding someone and digging him out in fifteen minutes is unlikely.

Avalanches can reach speeds of hundreds of miles an hour in only a few seconds. There are plenty of ways to reduce the risk of generating or getting caught in an avalanche. Get an avalanche report before you go to ensure that the weather and conditions are okay for the activity. Try not to hike through bowls or shuts, where avalanches usually happen. Don't hike on days that immediately follow heavy snowfalls or rain, or on warm days which increase the weight of the top layer of snow. Hike along tree lines that can provide some shelter from an avalanche. If you hear an avalanche, seek to get deeper into the trees on the high side of the slope. Also, check the slopes for fractures in the snow—this will be an indicator of instability—and snowballs that have rolled down a slope; these can indicate temperatures warm enough to cause destabilization. Carry beacons, trackers, and probes in case an avalanche happens. This way, people can find you. Test the snow to see if there are layers, or if the top layer is heavy or prone to slide. Finally, avoid hiking anywhere there is likelihood of a problem.

This information shouldn't be thought of as comprehensive. These are just examples of all I've learned over the years in winter camp training. Because of the training, winter camping has been a much more enjoyable and safe experience. It helped us to make good decisions.

Members of Troop 743 winter camping in the Wasatch Mountains where the boy slept in snow caves

Self-Discovery

Self-discovery is all about learning what kind of person you really are. The Boy Scouts offer the perfect chance for many young men to discover the character and values they want to present to the world, and to find strength and values they didn't know they possessed. When young men do hard things, such as fifty-mile backpack trips, it reveals strength they didn't know they possessed. I don't mean just physical strength, either, but mental strength, emotional strength, and strength of character. They are also required to perform leadership responsibilities as part of their rank requirements. Trying to be the leader of a youth group helps teach all the lessons that go along with leadership. I've seen many young men who may have ended up directionless or with bad character if it weren't for the activities and friendship they found through scouting, and the leadership chances they were given.

Participation in scouting exposes young men to hundreds of experiences not possible from any other sports program or club. One aspect of the varsity program is designed to personally develop career goals by visiting the offices of doctors, dentists, TV station producers, and various other professions. These activities often trigger interests that help boys later in choosing careers for the rest of their lives. Young men spend as much as dozens of hours in service every year, such as rebuilding goose nests or serving food at homeless shelters. These kinds of activities open their eyes to the world around them.

Finding Enjoyable Activities

There have been many times when a scout participates in an activity and likes it so much that it becomes a favorite activity for life. In one troop in which I volunteered was a boy whose family was reclusive. They lacked many outdoor interests and skills. One of our activities was a day hike up one of our local canyons a forty-minute drive from where we lived called Big Cottonwood Canyon. Big Cottonwood Canyon is home to two world-class ski resorts. By driving east over the ridge, one can drop down into Park City, where the Sundance Film Festival is held every year. The canyon is in the Wasatch Mountains east of the biggest cities in Utah. They rise up from the valley floor to 4,200 feet high and can be as large as 11,000 feet with steep slopes, various kinds of wildlife, and gorgeous scenery. The canyons are used for biking, hiking, mountain climbing, swimming, fishing, hunting, sightseeing, and skiing. There is even a granite quarry with a cave converted into a vault where records are stored.

The trailhead is located just past a double hairpin turn one third of the way up the canyon. The trail itself is 2.6 miles long and leads up the south slope of the mountain canyon. One mile up the trail is an outcropping of rocks eight hundred feet above the canyon floor. The view from here is quite astounding. The homebody father and son were extremely impressed. This was probably the first mountain hike they had been on. Afterward, it seemed that every few weeks they would find me to tell me about another hike on which they had gone.

Their hikes got longer and eventually included many of the Wasatch Mountains' peaks. I have witnessed this experience many times during my years in scouting. I have seen young men choose professions related to experiences in scouting, or embracing pastimes they have experienced in scouting. Young men learn about the things they really enjoy, and develop passions for activities they otherwise wouldn't have encountered or thought themselves capable of enjoying without the Boy Scouts.

Fifty-Mile Backpack through Lassen

Backpacker awareness training helps adult leaders plan and execute troop backpacking activities through high country. The important points focus on nutrition, first aid, safety, planning, preparation, equipment use, BSA requirements, types of clothing, and maintaining a lightweight backpack. The lighter the backpack, the less effort expended during the trip. The training has two parts: an in-class section and a hands-on section. This training is very useful and I would strongly suggest that a leader take this course before trying to plan a troop backpack trip. All the backpacking trips I've been on have been fun, but the one that was the most memorable was a fifty-mile backpack trip through Lassen National Park. Lassen is one of the most beautiful mountainous locations I have ever seen. The air smelled so fresh and the sky was so blue. There were pastures of green, waving grass, winding streams, and a background of majestic mountains covered in evergreen pines and Douglas firs. Flower-sprinkled grassy fields were lined by barbed-wire fences with wooden posts while the occasional picturesque wooden barn dotted the landscape. This is an active volcanic park, like Yellowstone. Some of the features we experienced were boiling mud pots, cinder cones, hot sulfur springs, cold boiling lakes, one of the tallest peaks in California, and of course beautiful mountain vistas. Lassen is fifty miles east of Redding, California, along Highway 44 and is considered part of the Cascade Range. It is forested with pines and firs, and includes many trout-filled lakes and streams. Warner Valley, marking the southern edge of the Lassen Plateau, features hot spring areas. This forested, steep valley also has large meadows that have wildflowers in spring.

My friend George Gettys was one of the other unit leaders and planned the fifty-mile backpack trip through the national park that started on a Monday and ended on a Saturday. George used a USGS TOPO program that was able to print daily maps and showed the trail with the elevation changes we would encounter compared to the distance we would travel. Having this information was helpful in the planning so that the elevation changes could be distributed throughout the week and not condensed into a single day or two. The USGS program could also be downloaded into a GPS unit to make sure we took the right forks in the trail. There had been situations when we didn't have a GPS and took the wrong trail because the fork wasn't very visible.

The week we went was perfect; the skies never clouded up, there was no rain, and the temperature was fairly mild. On Monday, we drove from Sacramento to Lassen National Park, which took four hours. This loss of time limited the distance we were able to hike to only a few miles. For this trip, we staged a car with more food so we didn't have to carry it all for the whole week. We left a truck in the parking lot at the base of Lassen, which would be part of our hiking trip on Thursday on our way to the south gate. Most of the boys complained about hiking that first day, even though it was only six miles.

From Tuesday through Friday, we hiked between ten and twelve miles per day. The second day was also filled with complaints of discomfort, but the third day I didn't hear a single complaint. I also found it interesting that not one boy needed to be asked to get up or to start preparing his breakfast. I have rarely had an experience where I have seen so much growth and maturity in young men in such a short period of time. They learned to be determined and do hard things, and they did it without complaining. I didn't hear another complaint the rest of the trip.

We hiked across a lava field on our way to the Cinder Cone, which rises up 750 feet to the rim and drops back down two hundred feet. We hiked the Cinder Cone on the way to Butte Lake, where we were camping for the night. That evening, one of the scoutmasters sneezed and we saw a ripple all the way across the lake. It turned out there were bugs on the water and the sound disturbed them. His sneezes were so loud, though, we wouldn't have been surprised if they caused the ripple all by themselves. While at Butte Lake, a group of backpackers came through and one of the female hikers had a severe blister on her foot. She had bought a new pair of boots for the hike and hadn't yet broken them in. One of the suggestions from HAT training is to soak boots in water, put them on, and wear them for a day. We had some mole skin in our adventure first-aid kit, so we fixed her up and gave her the rest of it for her trip. For hiking and backpacking trips, blisters are one of the most common injuries.

In addition to blisters, hyperthermia is a condition that should be of concern for scout leaders taking boys on hikes and backpacking trips. Hyperthermia is a condition where the body temperature rises two degrees above normal. Not staying hydrated can cause hyperthermia, since the body uses fluids such as sweat to cool itself. A person who is experiencing hyperthermia will most likely have the following symptoms: They will be hot, dry, disoriented, and possibly look redder in color. Treatments include getting the person to drink cool liquids, getting some shade, applying a wet compress, and letting him or her rest awhile. Our troop has found that requesting boys to bring hydration packs for hikes and backpack trips is a great way to keep boys hydrated. If a boy has to stop what he's doing to access his water bottle, he will most likely postpone drinking water.

We found a place that would have been great for treating hyperthermia. While hiking near Cold Boiling Lake, most of the adults jumped into the water and challenged the boys to do the same. I'm not sure what the temperature was, but after the boys felt the water, not one of them jumped in. I supposed they still had to work on being brave.

In the vehicle that we'd parked with food for the last part of the hike was an ice chest full of ice and two watermelons. Part of the trip included hiking up Lassen Peak. Two of the more athletic boys who were in training for football volunteered to carry the watermelons to the top of Lassen. Hiking Lassen was more of a treat since we left our backpacks at the car and were used to the altitude and hiking conditions. Even the boys carrying the watermelons seemed to make it up the climb with ease. At the top, we cut up the watermelons and shared with everyone on the top of the mountain, including other hikers not part of our troop. The view from the summit was amazing; we enjoyed a mostly clear blue sky and a view that seemed to extend over one hundred miles. After hiking down Lassen Peak, we stopped at the cars to replenish some supplies. From the parking lot we continued to the south entrance, where the trip ended. We loaded up and headed home.

Food for this trip consisted mostly of dehydrated foods, or foods where water is the main ingredient to produce a dish. As you can imagine, dehydrated foods aren't the most savory to eat but they give you the nutrition you need to survive. During this trip I was introduced to a backpacker oven that works on top of a backpacker stove. With this backpacker oven you can create pizza, cake, or almost anything you would normally bake in an oven. The restriction is that the oven volume is only one to one and a half quarts. To bake a cake, you would have to make two separate batches. The oven also comes with a tent and deflector shield to keep the heat from the stove confined around the oven. Of course, the tent and shield are not sealed so there is wasted heat and fuel. What's great about the oven is that the foods produced tend to be desirable to the scouts; you can barter your leftover cake for some product or service from them.

For those who have never done a fifty-mile backpack trip, I want to help give a better idea of the physical demands of such an activity. In the BSA, young men will determine how many paces it takes them to walk one hundred feet. A pace is the measure of distance when one foot hits the ground. If a scout uses twenty paces to go one hundred feet, he picks up and puts down his right or left foot twenty times to go one hundred feet. If we assume a young man's leg weighs five pounds, then a young man will have lifted 2.6 tons for each leg over the course of one mile. During a fifty-mile backpack trip, this equates to 20.6 tons per leg per day. When adding the effort to lift one's body weight and pack weight and the hundreds or thousands of feet in elevation, it's not hard to comprehend the physical exertion. Not knowing a body's physical capabilities or limits makes one always question if or when a scout might quit. Therefore, backpack trips like this, if accomplished, significantly develop a young man's determination as well as confidence.

Members of Troop 248 in a parking lot near Mount Tamalpias at the start of the 50 mile bike ride along Highway 1

COPE Course Challenges

East of Sacramento, an hour off Interstate 80, is a BSA camp known as Marin Sierra Scout Camp. It's halfway between Sacramento and Tahoe, so close to I-80 that I often heard the traffic. It's a beautiful camp with a small lake for waterfront activities. From the general look of the area one might conclude that the trees are mostly evergreens, but there is a significant quantity of oaks, maples, willows, and ash trees. The area has a rugged mountainous feel due to the many granite rock outcroppings mixed with the green picturesque vegetation. This was the scout camp that our troop usually attended and I have fond memories of it. The camp held at Marin Sierra was top notch because it was planned, organized, and supervised by some well-trained and dedicated leaders. For eight years our Boy Scout camp at Marin Sierra was set up by our stake leadership in partnership with adjoining stakes or units. Our stake scout leadership rented out this scout camp every year for the whole week to provide a stake-sponsored scout camp. The stake required each participating troop to provide volunteers, such as cooks, merit badge counselors, administrators, water-front directors, range directors, and cooking staff. As a result, the scout camp had great food, well-trained leadership, and quality programs for a lower cost. The merit badge counselors were well organized and professional, and sought to help the boys learn their materials and earn their badges. The stake leadership continually made adjustments and improvements to make this the best camp possible.

Generally it is a struggle to take a good shower at scout camp; either there are too few showers, they are not well maintained, the line is too long, or the water is cold. This camp had several shower stations that were always available and in many locations. They were twenty square feet with two-foot by four-foot walls covered in corrugated, galvanized metal panels. Each shower station contained a dozen nozzles and since the water tank was huge, there was always a shower open. There were no roofs, so it felt like taking a shower out in the open. The only trouble was getting hot water. The hot water was heated by wood fires under two- to three-hundred-gallon water tanks that would take four hours to get warm enough for a decent shower.

I have attended dozens of scout camps over the years and I must say that the food provided at this stake-run camp was the best I have ever encountered. Two or three adult staff members were in charge of the kitchen for the week, and three adult troop staff members ran it each day. Because all the staff members were volunteers, more money was spent on food. Friday night's dinner was a traditional Thanksgiving turkey with stuffing, mashed potatoes, and gravy. Another dinner consisted of barbequed hamburgers, and the kitchen staff provided dry-ice root beer, which was awesome. Some of the other favorite foods included barbequed chicken, pepperoni calzones, and breakfast burritos. After the camp-wide nightly fire, a troop representative could stop by the kitchen to pick up a treat for the troop such as cookies and milk or Rice Krispies treats. There was also a candy jar each day for boys to guess how many items were inside. Whoever guessed closest would win the candy jar. Of course, the winner was asked to share it with the troop.

The scout camp COPE course director mostly built the course and manned it for the whole week every year that I can remember our stake camp going there. As part of our stake's rental agreement of the camp, our stake was required to make improvements. Every year, one or two attractions were added to the COPE course. Ken Hazelbaker, the director, was able to get the materials donated and spent a week of his vacation every year before scout camp to upgrade or add events. To have the course pass BSA requirements, the COPE course manager is required to train at a BSA facility, which takes at least a week. This selfless individual gave up two to three weeks of vacation every year.

Ken had a vision of how the COPE course could be used to help boys overcome fear so it could be replaced with confidence. He called his course the Know Fear course. His attractions were physically and mentally challenging, difficult to accomplish, and many required study, planning, and team-work. Before each event, some inspirational thought or scrip-tures were given to provide understanding and encouragement.

Ken Hazelbaker was employed by a company to provide safety systems during hazardous construction projects that required wire cables and harnesses. George Gettys and I were usually at scout camp as leaders for the troop, but when the boys were at merit badge class, we would help Ken set up the Know Fear course and work on his new features. Ken spent the rest of the year with his own troop. When Van Vleck Ranch property in Rancho Murieta, California, was donated to the BSA, Ken spent a month there installing two four-hundred-foot zip lines and a one-hundred-foot, four-sided climbing tower with three sides for climbing and one side for rappelling.

Every weekend, he directed a dozen volunteers to accomplish the work.

Ken is a real character. Since our camp was usually on the Fourth of July, he would dress up like Captain America with a cape that looked like the US flag. He would put on a climbing hat, harness, and attach lots of belays, carabiners, and a climbing rope over his shoulder. At the flag ceremony in the evening, he would run up front with all those metal attachments clanging and sing an adapted version of the *Pinocchio* tune "Hi-Diddle-Dee-Dee (*Know Fear* the Life for Me)!" He was seriously involved in scouting. If we ever wanted to find a new place to go, he always had a good suggestion. He was always willing to go the extra mile, because he cared about the boys and saw how the scout program would help them.

Ken came up with several tasks for the boys. For example, the trust fall involved a boy standing on the edge of a picnic table and falling backward into the arms of six to eight boys lined up in two rows facing each other. This took a lot of faith in the boys who were going to catch him. About 50% of those who tried failed. When I was young, we tried this activity standing on the ground and falling backward only a couple of feet into the catcher's arms.

The confidence pole was another great challenge. This was a fifteen-foot-high tree trunk with the top cut off and spikes nailed into it to form a ladder. All activities where boys were more than eight feet off the ground required top roping to a full-body harness attached to them. They would climb the tree and try to stand on the top. The area on which they could stand was not that big, probably only eight inches in diameter. You can imagine it was quite difficult to get on top of the trunk without anything to hold on to while climbing up from the spikes. After balancing on top of the tree, the boys would jump out five feet to a trapeze and then let go. The rope belayer would ease them back to the ground.

Another task for the boys was the high beam. This required them to climb a rope ladder up to a beam tied between two trees twenty feet off the ground. A rope ladder is difficult and unstable, since no part of it is rigid. When you apply pressure to a rope rung, it slips to the side. After climbing the ladder, the boys would walk across the beam from one tree to the next and back to the middle. From there, they would jump off the beam and the belayer eased them back to the ground.

The V-cables were a lot of fun. Two cables were attached to one tree from two other trees, forming a V. Two boys would each stand on a cable at the close end of the V and hold hands. They would work their way down to the wide end of the V, applying pressure to each other between their hands. There was no way for the boys to get to the wide end without leaning forward and applying pressure against each other. It took a lot of practice before both participants trusted each other enough to make it to the wide end of the cables.

Ken also had a zip line and a rappelling station. Personally, I don't find a zip line all that scary. Backing over a cliff with a rope in your hand to rappel down it can be pretty intimidating for the first time, though. I have rarely seen anyone step up to the edge who wasn't at least a little scared. Many boys required several attempts before they would try it. Doing hard things, overcoming one's fears, and building confidence were the objectives of the Know Fear course.

Campfires were a highlight due to the traditions fostered by the directors. The campfires were well planned, organized, and attended. For many years, the camp director arranged local actors to come up to portray significant characters from US or religious history and perform a scene or sketch about an important event. Platforms, towers, and other props were constructed and used to add realism to the depiction.

One year, a small cable-and-pulley system was set up for a fire lighting ceremony. The ends of the cable system went from the fire pit up into a nearby tree at a forty-five-degree angle. A scout dressed like a Native American performed a rain dance around the fire pit, after which someone lit an accelerant-soaked rag tied to the cable. The rag was propelled into the fire pit to light the fire. It was a pretty cool demonstration.

Friday afternoon of scout camp was the Scout Olympics, when troops and scouts get to show off how proficient they are with basic scout skills, including first aid, fire building, knot tying, orienteering, and a troop-versus-troop tug-of-war. All events are timed and the first troop to complete the task correctly with the fastest time wins that event. There are points for first, second, and third places. The first-aid event requires a team of scouts to properly treat a scout with multiple injuries. They must address the injuries in order of seriousness, and provide the correct treatments. For fire building, the team of scouts must build a fire, set a can filled with a couple of cups of water on it, and bring the water to a boil. Knot tying has six scouts see how fast each can tie a given knot connecting sections of rope, tying it to a log, and suspending the log over a horizontal pole, then affixing the other end of the rope to a tree. The orienteering challenge is timed and graded according to a Silva compass course on numbered markers. The grade is how close the scout team gets to the correct numbered marker. Finally, there's the tug of war. It doesn't need an explanation, but it is a lot of fun.

In addition to the scout challenges, there is a scoutmaster canoe race that is very entertaining. A scout leader sits at each end of the canoe to maneuver it while a scout sits in the middle trying to fill the canoe up with water with a bucket. The leaders need to paddle the canoe around a course to a finish line before the canoe is full of water. Some of the leaders are quite proficient at canoeing, which usually causes the scout to simply flip the canoe near the finish line out of frustration. These Scout Olympics help the boys review their scout skills and encourage them to develop teamwork. Many of these challenges cannot be successful without the group working together as a team.

Overcoming Fear

Taking Highway 49 south out of Auburn, California, for 2.5 miles brings you to a bridge that crosses the American River and a dirt road that parallels the river. Around 1.25 miles east on the dirt road is the oldest part of a rock quarry that has been used for years by rock climbers. It was used in the movie *XXX* for a scene in which the main character, Xander (played by Vin Diesel), steals a Corvette from a senator, drives it off the bridge, and crashes it at the bottom of Auburn Ravine. This is a great location. When you climb up the rock hills, you can see up and down the ravine, cut out by the river, and the Sierra foothills.

The walls of the quarry are ideal for climbing because many of the rock walls are perfectly vertical. Over the years, rock climbers have installed permanent anchors all over the quarry. Right at the entry is a wall that gradually inclines from the quarry floor and is seventy feet high. This wall allows beginning climbers any length of route to practice. The farther into the quarry you go, the higher the walls get. We had a couple of ropes that were 160 feet long but weren't long enough for some of the walls.

Most of the time we went to the quarry, we would rappel down the first rock wall that was seventy feet high. Trying to encourage young men to rappel of a cliff is difficult because it is scary to put trust in people and equipment with which one may not be familiar. At the top of the rock wall ten feet from the edge is a drill rod that seemed permanently attached to the rock. We would tie our ropes to it, and young men would put on a harness with a belay and carabiner attached to the front. The rope would be fed through the belay and carabiner, which would be locked. Each climber would grab the taut line in one hand and the slack line in the other, and whoever was climbing would start backing over the edge. Right at the edge is where it is the scariest, when you're looking over the cliff edge and the ground is seventy feet down. You know if any piece of the equipment fails, you're probably dead. But once you're over the edge and your weight is held by the rope, your fear goes away. Even after you have done it once, doing it the next time is still a little scary.

It helps to practice on walls that are short. Our church had a cinder block wall around its property that was seven feet tall and perfect for practicing. Young men need to confront their fears, which is what makes this such a great activity. If they accept the challenge and rappel down the wall, their confidence grows significantly. When kids succeed in overcoming a significant challenge, their joy is hard to contain.

Members of Troop 248 rappelling down a 70' wall in an old Rock Quarry

Kings Peak

Kings Peak is located on the north slope of the Uinta mountain range and is the highest peak in Utah. To get there requires a minimum hike of sixteen miles with a change of elevation of more than five thousand feet. Our path was to hike the Henry's Fork Trail to Dollar Lake, camp there for the night, hike to Kings Peak the next day, and return to Dollar Lake. On the last day of the trip, we would hike out to the Henry's Fork Trail parking lot and drive home. The hike from Henry's Fork Trail to Dollar Lake is seven miles with twelve hundred feet of elevation change. The elevation of Dollar Lake is near the tree line, meaning that not many trees grow above this elevation. Most of the hike to Kings Peak is above the tree line. Hiking from Dollar Lake to Kings Peak and back is eighteen miles, with close to four thousand feet of elevation difference. From Dollar Lake, the trail rises eleven hundred feet to Gunsight Pass where the trail starts as dirt and transitions to mostly rock. At the top of Gunsight Pass are two trails: one that drops down into Painter Basin and rises back up to Anderson Pass, and another that leads through a boulder field southwest to Anderson Pass. The Painter Basin trail loses five hundred feet of elevation which must be regained going back up to Anderson Pass. This trail is one and a half miles longer but is the safest trail to Kings Peak. From Anderson Pass to the top of Kings Peak is a distance of a mile and another eight hundred feet of elevation. It's difficult to hike more than a dozen yards or so without stopping and catching one's breath.

It rains most summer afternoons in the Uintas. As a result, the Henry's Fork Basin is green and vibrant with flowers that time of year. Rock structures in the area are made of quartz, slate, and shale of various colors but mostly red to dark gray. As mentioned earlier, many mountains with a reddish color provide an awesome contrast to the blue skies and green plant life. From Kings Peak you can see down into at least five of the basins in the Uinta range, at least one hundred miles. The scenery close by is the most desired.

Many people get altitude sickness because their bodies are not used to the lack of oxygen. Symptoms of altitude sickness include headache, nausea, lack of energy, no desire to eat or drink, and dizziness. This happened to me on this trip. I was able to hike into Dollar Lake and made it almost to Anderson Pass before the symptoms of altitude sickness started to set in. I pushed my body to the edge and discovered I had moved beyond the limits I once had.

A Member of Troop 473 after hiking to the tallest Peak in Utah (13,527')

Dillon's Beach Campouts

One of the most popular activities we did as a troop was camping at Dillon's Beach. The boys enjoyed it so much that we would plan to camp there at least once every year and sometimes twice. Dillon's Beach is south of Bodega Bay and north of Point Reyes National Seashore. South of Dillon's Beach is a camping area called Lawson's Landing that provides open-area camping on grass-covered fields where cows are allowed to roam and feed. This means that you need to be careful of where you put your tent. Part of Lawson's Landing includes a boat launch, a pier, and a large flat and calm beach. The south end of the beach is calm because it is sheltered from the open ocean by land jutting out from the Point Reyes National Seashore that encloses Tamales Bay. This part of the beach has a mild decline into the ocean, and when the tide goes out, the beach grows by several hundred feet. From the coast, the terrain inclines up to a plateau several hundred feet high. Most of the land is fenced with green grass and some trees, usually eucalyptus.

The wind is almost always blowing; as a result, many people fly kites there. On one scout trip, I had driven there in a Geo Metro that had wing windows in the back. After playing in the dunes for a couple of hours, we returned to find the two wing windows ripped off and on the ground. The wind had been gusting and had broken the plastic latches.

Since Dillon's Beach has a parking lot, we were able to bring about anything to make camp more enjoyable. Therefore, we brought Dutch ovens for cooking. What would Boy Scout camping be like without Dutch oven cooking? You can cook almost anything with one, from roasts to rolls and cakes. George Gettys liked to make homemade barbeque beans in his. He would start by cutting up and cooking one pound of bacon in the bottom until it was brown, then add onions and cook them until they were caramelized. Then he'd add various cans of beans, mustard, ketchup, and brown sugar. They tasted awesome. The trick to cooking with a Dutch oven is to know how many briquettes to use. At Wood Badge we learned that one briquette provides 25°F of cooking heat. If you need 400°F to cook something, you need sixteen briquettes distributed between the top and bottom of the oven.

Horseneck clams are popular in this area. The shells can be as big as softballs and the necks can be two to three feet long. To dig them out, most people use a three-foot-long clam tube and a shovel. After the tide goes out, look for a squirt of water into the air, and then find the hole from which the water squirted. Center the tube over the hole and push it down into the sand until just the handles are sticking up. Now start digging out the sand in the tube with a shovel and be careful not to cut off the neck of the clam, since the neck is good meat for eating.

Fishing for crabs from the pier is also a popular activity; all one needs is a crab net, twenty-five feet of rope, and some bait. Tie the bait to the center of the net, tie the rope to the net, and throw the net into the water. After a few minutes, pull the net up and see if you have anything.

On the north shore of the beach are some outcroppings of rocks, and when the tides go out, many tide pools are formed. I love playing in tide pools, looking for sea creatures like crabs, starfish, anemones, and sea snails.

Members of Troop 248 on a Pier at Dillion's Beach doing some crabbing

Lake Oroville Floating Campsite

Oroville Lake is located north of Sacramento along Highway 65 some ninety miles on the edge of the Sierra foothills. It is east of the city of Oroville by eight to ten miles. At Lake Oroville are several two-story floating campsites available to rent. The capacity of a floating campsite is fifteen people, and it has a barbeque, restroom, picnic table, a covered living area, and an upper deck for sleeping. The campsite is accessible only by boat and is allowed to have only three boats moored to it. This lake has some of the best amenities of any state park I've visited. In addition to all of the boating activities, there are many hiking and biking trails, as well as cliff jumping, swimming, fishing, horseback riding, and golfing. Around the lake are ten boat launches and more than a dozen regular campgrounds. The lake is more than twenty-five square miles and, due to the mild California climate, the park is open all year round.

Lake Oroville's floating campsites are great places for boy scouts to camp, and they have all the readily available facilities. The boys won't get as dirty since they won't have to sleep on the ground or camp in a regular campground. I highly recommend this place.

Members of Troop 248 camping on a floating camp site at Lake Oroville

Building and Launching Rockets

Over the years I have had a tradition at Christmas to buy my kids a model rocket that they could build. Of course, I would have to buy and build one for myself, too. We have amassed and lost quite a collection of rockets, from small rockets with no recovery systems to large, six-foot-tall rockets. Some have dropped bombs while others carried cameras and "astronauts" (insects). Model rocket motors are classed by letter, and then rated with numbers. The alpha character indicates the class or impulse power, the first number indicates the thrust, and the second number indicates the delay before the recovery charge ignition. Model-rocket motor classification only extends to class G; anything larger is considered a high-powered rocket motor.

When we moved to California, George was into rockets also, so he and I enjoyed rocket building together. Since George was the merit badge counselor for space exploration, our hobby migrated over to the scout troop. George would provide the science and history of rockets during a weeknight troop activity. Then, on another weeknight, our troop built the rockets together as a group. Then, on some Saturday morning, we would get together over at the high school parking lot or a ball field and launch the rockets. We would allow the boy who owned the rocket to set it up with a motor and igniter, place it on the launch pad, hook up the igniter source, and launch the rocket. Afterward, the chase would be on to see who could get to the rocket first and catch it.

88

Jeff Johnson

Sam, one of the other scout leaders, bought a rocket that inflated with air called the Dude. It was made of silver Mylar which stood seven feet tall. It looked more like a real rocket when it was launched.

When I moved back to Utah, I became the merit badge counselor and have carried on this tradition. Many parents have shown up on launch day and, after seeing how much fun the boys had, asked if I could provide this activity during birthday parties.

Members of Troop 743 right before they launch the rockets that they have just finished building

Loon Lake: Puddle Stomper

My interest in winter camp started shortly after I moved to the Sacramento area. I was asked to work in the scouting troop as the varsity coach, and shortly thereafter I was invited to participate with the scouts and eleven-year-old boys at a winter camp. At the time, the eleven-year-old scouts and the regular scout troop were seasoned, and they had planned an extended winter camp up by Loon Lake in the Sierras for a week. Loon Lake's elevation is just short of seven thousand feet, and during late December it usually snows. For this camp, it rained the whole time! The camp was well planned, organized, and executed. The leader of the eleven-year-olds had winter survival training, so he had provided provisions that made the camp comfortable and enjoyable. When I was a young scout, the winter camps were barely survivable, let alone enjoyable.

One provision was a cardboard oven. A heavy cardboard box is cut on three edges of one face so that the contents of the box can be removed. This face now becomes the door of the oven. The interior is lined with aluminum foil. Additional cardboard pieces are cut and covered with aluminum to add another layer of insulation to the inside oven walls. A rack is made to allow a tray of briquettes or wood coals and a tray to hold the food while it is being cooked. Because of this oven we ate hot food every day, like baked potatoes and cake. This was some of the best food I have ever eaten on a campout, let alone a winter camp. The cake was made from a gingerbread mix with pears mixed in. The leader called them brown bears. It was an awesome-tasting cake, and was very moist.

Another provision was a fire tent, which was a series of tarps tied together and to surrounding trees to make them look like a tent with a gap between the roof and the walls of one foot. There was a fire barrel in the center, and everyone sat in camp chairs around the inside perimeter of the tent. It was so warm in there we didn't need to wear coats. During free time, the boys enjoyed building snowmen, sledding down the hill, and rolling three-foot snowballs down the hill. Because of all the rain, we spent most of the time inside the fire tent. My ideas about winter camping significantly improved because of that experience. Also, if a scout camps more than five days in the rain in a given year, he earns the Puddle Stomper patch. After this campout, the boys earned it.

Loon Lake Winter Camp

Loon Lake was one of the most popular places for us to winter camp due to the elevation, the closeness to Sacramento, the facilities, and the need for the electric company to keep the road open to monitor the conditions of the lake. I have winter camped at Loon Lake almost a dozen times. Three of those times we have been rained on. On one occasion, we arrived early enough to build an igloo, but due to the rain the structure failed during the night. In the middle of the night I noticed the roof caving, so I propped it up with two snow shovels until morning. After we cleared our equipment out of the igloo, I took out the shovels and the roof collapsed.

When I was the leader of the eleven-year-olds in the Sacramento area, we rented a chalet that is right next to the lake and built an igloo just outside it. Only a few of us stayed in the igloo that night. One of the safety issues of winter camps is making sure the boys drink enough water. Most people don't feel thirsty when it's cold. Water performs several vital functions, and if regular water intake is not happening, the body's ability to stay warm is compromised. One nice attribute about the chalet is that it has a clothes dryer for clothes that get wet from winter activities. The chalet is also heated, which makes it a safe house when young, inexperienced scouts attend. The chalet has three levels: downstairs are some bunks for sleeping, the main floor is the main activity area that can also be used for sleeping bags, and upstairs is a loft that is mostly used for sleeping.

Sons of Liberty

During the summer of 2004 there was a regional three-day scout camp at Van Vleck Ranch called the Sons of Liberty. Van Vleck Ranch is just outside of Rancho Murieta in California and is mostly open country with a few outcroppings of oak trees and yellow field grass. This time of year in the Sacramento area there is little chance of rain, and for the period of the camp it was sunny with blue skies every day. The property at Van Vleck Ranch was donated to the BSA sometime before 2004, and shortly afterward improvements started being made that would serve the Sons of Liberty camp and future scout camps.

More than two hundred fifty troops were in attendance, meaning there were several thousand individuals. I've heard that every year twenty thousand boy scouts attend a camp on the property. The camp has been permanently improved with two four-hundred-foot zip lines, a one-hundred-foot-tall climbing and rappelling tower, and an archery range. When we attended the Sons of Liberty, several above-ground pools were brought in so the boys could experience scuba diving. Temperatures in the area were 100°F and above and there wasn't much shade or wind. Because of the dust being kicked up by the several thousand people walking between events, most people were caked in dirt. You could imagine what the pool water looked like after a couple of days of hundreds of dirty kids getting in and out of it.

Beale AFB Jamb-O-Rama

North of Sacramento is Beale Air Force Base, which is a fairly remote location not close to any major towns. This base houses some of the air force's spy planes like the U2 and the SR-71. Back in the late spring of 1999, the Golden Empire Council held a Jamb-O-Rama there. This was a seriously exciting camp for me because my uncle was a design engineer on the SR-71 and had sent me every published article about that plane over the years. After the plane had been decommissioned and some of the data on it released, he attended a backpack trip with our scout troop. He spent three hours around the campfire telling stories about the plane.

The country around Beale AFB is flat with mildly rolling hills to the east covered in grass and oak trees. To the south of the building and tarmac are open fields where the scouts were allowed to set up their camps. On Friday evening, a concert was held and an inspirational speaker gave a presentation. He was an Eagle Scout who had won an X Games climbing competition for being the fastest person to climb a one-hundred-foot climbing tower. They showed footage from the competition and it looked like he was running up the wall. He spoke about an experience he had climbing the Matterhorn shortly after he won the X Games. He had been hiking a ridge line when the group he had been with encountered a glacier. He was tired and having trouble climbing the glacier when another climber advised him to stop and put on his crampons. The point of the story was that many people sometimes don't think clearly and need to listen to those people around them with a better perspective.

The military provides a liaison officer at each of their installations that scout leaders can contact about using their facilities for scout activities. Scouting groups are given special consideration and are usually allowed a place to stay overnight and almost the full use of a facility, such as cafeterias, tours, bowling lanes, movie theaters, etc. The scouts on this trip were not allowed near the buildings and tarmac until midday when they scheduled time to tour aircrafts near the runway and air show. The air force had a helicopter and a transport plane that the boys could climb in, and they had an SR-71 to look at from a distance.

When the air show started, the first plane that took off was a U2. Wow, was that plane noisy! Second was the SR-71, which was up and gone before we knew it. It flew high into the sky and turned on some smoke so we could see how fast it was flying, which was pretty cool. According to the schedule, an F-117 was supposed to have been in the air show, but due to a crash the week before in the UK, the plane was grounded. To make up for the F-117 grounding, the air force brought in a B-2 bomber. It didn't take off or land at Beale; it flew by fifty feet over the runway. I was amazed at how quiet and slow that plane flew. It looked like it was only flying at sixty miles an hour, and all I heard was a whirring noise. At the end of the show, the Blue Angels flew over and performed a few maneuvers. I don't know about the kids, but I sure had a good time.

Mountain Biking the Rubicon

West of Loon Lake is one of the entrances to the Rubicon Trail. The Rubicon Trail is a twenty-two-mile-long jeep trail that extends from Georgetown to South Lake Tahoe and borders the north end of the Desolation Wilderness. Desolation Wilderness is probably one of the most popular and well-used wildernesses in California, partly due to its ease of access, beautiful scenery, and location near populous towns. There are many lakes, campgrounds, and cabins for rent and trails to hike in addition to the Rubicon Trail. The Rubicon is so popular because of the many granite rock obstacles it has. When you combine a mountain atmosphere with camping, fishing, and rock crawling, you have an unbeatable weekend. Our trip was a little different, since our objective was to ride mountain bikes in the Granite Bowl obstacle and along the trail.

We camped on the south side of the lake. Just like the red sandstone in Moab, Utah, granite rock is fun to ride a bike on, and if it is free of debris, the traction is good. When we weren't riding along the Rubicon Trail, we were riding around the Granite Bowl. The Granite Bowl is right next to Loon Lake and it looks like a rock quarry.

It was fun to sit and watch rock crawlers try to outwit the rock structures. We saw some drivers misjudge the situation, roll their vehicles, and spend forty-five minutes trying to get unstuck from the rocks. It was also fun to see homemade rock crawlers that people had brought in an attempt to make a superior crawler. We saw one crawler that was hinged in the middle and had solid front and back axles like a front-end-loader tractor. It had a six-cylinder diesel engine that drove a hydraulic pump to drive the wheels, like most tractors. In addition, the crawler was water tight, and if the water was too deep for the wheels to get traction, the hydraulic power could be applied to a propeller and the crawler would work like a boat.

Pigeon Point Lighthouse

Pigeon Point Lighthouse is located on the California coast fifty miles south of San Francisco and has a campground nearby. Many of the usual activities are available here, but touring the lighthouse is fun. It is amazing to learn how lighthouses worked many years ago with Fresnel lenses and high-powered bulbs. When we camped there in the spring, gray whales were migrating up the coast in herds and we could see groups of blow spouts. It seemed that the whales were not more than a few hundred feet from the beach.

While we were camping at Pigeon Point, a fellow riding a road bike covered in packs stopped at the campground for the night. It looked like he hadn't had a bath or shaved in a month and his clothes were dirty. He said he had been biking for almost a month and had lost almost thirty pounds.

Presidio Camping

Along the coast on both sides of San Francisco Bay are World War II ammunition batteries that were built to help protect the bay from enemy activity. Three of them used to be available to rent for camping purposes and were maintained by the Presidio, a park and former military base, but operated by the San Francisco Recreation and Parks Department. Due to the age and disintegration of the facilities, they have since been shut down. One of these batteries is on Baker Beach, which is close to the south side of the Golden Gate Bridge. Cannons and ammunition were located along the coast to fire upon enemy ships. The battery at Baker Beach had mounts for four cannons; one of them was still mounted and fired one Saturday a month. These types of cannons can fire a projectile twenty-five miles out to sea.

Camping at the ammunition battery at Baker Beach is extremely fun because there are so many things to do within a short distance. Camping inside one of the batteries is quite interesting, since the concrete is twelve inches thick and dirt is put on top of it. The doors are heavy iron, and once closed, it is completely pitch black inside. There are lights, but when the lights were out, we couldn't see without a flashlight. At the Presidio is a bowling alley, park, and cafeteria. You can always play in the water or on the beach, but most of the time the water is cold. We always enjoyed playing Frisbee golf or capture the flag.

One of the best places to go in San Francisco is the Exploratorium. It has probably a hundred electrical, magnetic, optical, acoustic, biological, or physical demonstrations. When we visited the Exploratorium, we would spend hours there. The Exploratorium is a place to encourage youths to explore the sciences. It's also fun to walk around Chinatown and Fisherman's Wharf. There are several blocks of Chinese shops and restaurants in Chinatown. Most of the shops sell products from China. Fisherman's Wharf is part of the port of San Francisco where ships used to come from all over the world to dock and unload their goods. Most of those occupations have been moved to a new dock farther into the bay, but boats that bring in fish for sale still use this part of the port. Fresh fish is still for sale at Pier 39. The main street is also loaded with shirt and souvenir shops, museums, charter boats, and restaurants.

One of the activities we tried was hiking across the Golden Gate Bridge just to say we did it. Halfway across, we stopped to watch the variety of boats coming and going, including the occasional large cruise ship and large shipping vessels. There is usually a good current going in or out depending on the tide, and there is always a stiff wind. At the south base of the bridge is Fort Mason, which was constructed in 1864 to defend the bay. The facility had twelve cannons; six of them were ten inches wide and could fire a cannonball a couple of miles.

HAT: Paddle Sports

Paddle Sports is training for adult leaders to plan and execute the troop activity of running a river with canoes or kayaks. The training covers trip planning, equipment use, water craft maneuvers, BSA requirements, safety, rescue, reading a river, and first aid. The training has two parts, an in-class section that takes place at a community college and a hands-on section that takes place over one weekend at a lake and a river. The in-class portion is typically held on a Friday night and Saturday and covers the critical requirements for conducting a safe and successful river run. Topics include clothing, paddle strokes, maneuvers, reading the river, communication signs, first aid, trip planning, and rescues.

After our hands-on section, my class spent the weekend learning and practicing the maneuvers at a lake on Saturday and putting those skills to use by running a river on Sunday. Our river experience was in the middle part of the Tuolumne River. The Tuolumne River is a large river, but the middle section doesn't have any rapids. The water is deep and moves a discharge volume of two thousand five hundred to four thousand cubic feet per second. Of course, the highest rates are during the spring runoff season. The trip took five hours and we practiced the skills of reading the river, paddle strokes, maneuvers, rescues, and communication signs. Having an outdoor adventure without having to worry about kids getting lost or hurt was an awesome experience.

Salmon Fishing the Sacramento River

In the late fall, when the river water temperature drops below 60°F, the king salmon run begins in the Sacramento and American Rivers near Sacramento, California. Late fall in Sacramento means the skies are clear and average temperatures in the morning are in the mid-50s with highs in the mid-70s. This time of year, the color of the water can have a reddish hue because of the quantity of king salmon migrating upstream to spawn. When the salmon really start to run, the fish weir racks are inserted across the river to force the salmon to swim up the fish ladder into the hatchery. I can remember some years when the banks of the river were covered in dead fish.

On Hazel Avenue in Sacramento, the California Department of Fish and Wildlife manage the Nimbus Fish Hatchery to spawn, incubate, and raise salmon and steelhead trout to be released back into the river system. The hatchery has twelve cement ponds to raise the fish for six months to a year until they are large enough to go into the river. The ponds are covered with nets to prevent birds from feasting on the young fry. In the pond area you can buy handfuls of fish food to feed the fish; it is fun to watch the frenzy when you throw in the whole handful.

When the salmon start to run, there is a line of fishermen with hip waders fishing for salmon just below the Nimbus Dam. When the salmon enter the river system to spawn, they generally do not eat, so fishing for salmon is usually done with spinners and jigs that annoy the fish and cause them to bite at the lure.

Two of the scout leaders in our troop are serious fishermen and go fishing for salmon at least once a week. It's convenient to fish for salmon in Sacramento because the river runs right through the middle of town from north to south. Their method of fishing for salmon is to drive upstream one quarter of a mile and troll downstream using spinners at a slow speed. When they're done trolling, they reel in their lines, drive back up, put their lines back in, and do it again. This has proven to be a successful way for them to catch salmon. Most of the time fishing is just sitting in a chair, listening to music, and snacking.

Our troop scheduled a fishing trip at Garcia Bend of the Sacramento River when my son Adam was an eleven-year-old scout. I was in one boat and he was in the other. Within a couple hours, Adam and two other boys in his boat had caught fish. At the time, Adam probably weighed fifty pounds, and the fish he caught weighed thirty-two pounds. When the fish resisted, Adam started to go overboard. Luckily, the scout leader was able to grab the waistband of his pants before he was pulled too far. Adam could hardly hold up the fish, even resting it on his belly. I didn't catch anything that trip. The next year, Adam caught a fifty-four-pound salmon and I caught a seventeen-pound fish. You can imagine who the fisherman of the family is.

**Members of Troop 248 after a day of fishing for Salmon on
the Sacramento River**

University Falls

University Falls is a granite rock formation east of Georgetown, California, where a stream of water flows to make four natural water slides. To get to the falls, you need to park by a gate off the main road and hike two to three miles farther east. The hike is mostly on a dirt road until you get within a couple hundred yards of the falls, where the trail narrows and gets steep in some areas. The falls are in the foothills of California and used to be fairly heavily forested until some loggers started harvesting the lumber. Now there are patches of somewhat bare hills. The rock structures that make up the falls are mostly solid granite, making the surface continuous. The water that flows over the rock allows a thin coating of moss or something organic to grow, making the surface slick. Almost every time we have been there, someone has slipped and fallen.

For the first three water slides, the water flows over the rock and drops into pools of water. The first rolls over the rock at a slight angle and from a height of twelve to fifteen feet. The next couple are higher, and the rock cuts back near their pools, allowing someone to drop vertically into the water. The last fall is more of a channel carved into the rock with many curves and obstructions, making it difficult to safely navigate. Many people have taken the plunge successfully, but others have been injured. The water is chilly, which has discouraged many from engaging in the fun.

Activities that take place at University Falls have always been on a Saturday early morning. Most summer Saturdays in northern California are warm and clear with partly high-atmo-sphere-cloudy skies. What better activity is there on a summer Saturday morning than playing in a natural water park?

Members of Troop 248 sliding over granite structures at University Falls.

Reflections on Thirty Years in Scouting

I want to provide some suggestions about things to do and things not to do as I look back over my thirty years of adult leadership in scouting.

Take the BSA training at all levels as soon as you can. This will ensure that you're running the program correctly and safely. Make sure that all of the other adult leaders have training, too. This is especially important for high-adventure activities. The HAT training provides good ideas about conducting high-adventure activities to prevent unnecessary injury or loss. When I was a young scout leader, I took some boys on a backpacking trip before I had backpacking training, and there were two important things I didn't do. The first was to evaluate the boys' hiking ability before doing the backpacking trip, and the second was to review what the kids had brought for the trip to determine if each pack was too heavy for the boy to carry for many miles.

On another trip, I worked with a young, inexperienced scout leader not familiar with the rules of safe hiking in groups. He was at the front of the line and I was at the back, and he hiked so fast that the boys in between us were strung out. One of the boys in the middle took the wrong fork in the trail and was lost for several hours. It is good to review the rules of an activity with the boys and the leaders before it gets underway to avoid situations like this. Buy and use a pair of walkie-talkies. Ensure the kids have copies of the map and compasses and know how to use them. They should also carry whistles to be able to signal for help.

For winter camping activities, it's a good idea to have winter camp training every year before winter camp. It takes two to three times and several bad choices before the kids start to get the hang of it. It's also a good idea to invite the parents to the training so they can ensure the boy packs the right gear; it helps them know what quality gear requirements are. It also gives the parents ideas for birthday and Christmas presents, since they can buy their boys the items they need to fill in whatever gaps exist in their gear. In addition, it's a good idea to have a review meeting after winter camp, ask the boys about the good and bad experiences they had, and what could have been done to improve their experiences. This helps the boys think about the choices they made and makes them more aware of the consequences of their choices.

When I was an adult, many times I would get frustrated with the boys for not following through in their leadership responsibilities, so I went ahead and took over. That was not a good idea; it's important for the boys to be in charge even if they fail. If they fail, then they will learn. If an adult takes over, then they feel they don't have ownership of their leadership responsibilities. The best way to handle such a situation would be with patience and maybe a one-on-one talk to review their decisions and ask what they would suggest to make them better. Also, make sure you compliment them on the good things they do.

One thing a leader should know is that the boys really do listen, even if it doesn't appear that they do. Not only are they listening, but they appreciate the sacrifices you are making. I can't tell you how many times I have had a conversation with someone who was one of my scouts many years earlier and he expressed gratefulness for the activities and what he learned. Scouts truly value your friendship. Many of them continue to communicate the significant experiences in their lives, even when they get older.

Plan activities that are fun; if you're having fun, they will have fun. Plan activities that you know how to do. If you don't know how to do a new skill that a particular activity requires, invite someone you know who has that skill to share it with your troop.

Training at all levels of leadership, such as the committee members, chairman, and charter representative, help a troop run well. Have parents participate on the troop committee, get them involved, and they will always know what is going on. If parents aren't on the troop committee, they should at least attend the committee meetings so they can stay informed and make sure the activities their boy needs to progress are getting scheduled. Sending emails between all the troop participants and parents will also allow good communication if not all parents are able to attend scout meetings.

For the last thirty or so years, I have worked in a corporate environment where I have interviewed and hired employees. Many companies focus their interview questions toward the technical requirements of a job and tend to neglect other important characteristics that portray values and ethics such as whether or not a candidate is hardworking, honest, on time, healthy, and friendly, as well as dozens of other similar characteristics. Employers sometime forget the importance of these kinds of characteristics. I have seen many employees who have great technical understanding but poor values and ethics. I have asked my kids to imagine themselves as business owners and make a list of the qualities they would look for in an employee. I would encourage them to acquire those values themselves as a way of making themselves more marketable to employers.

I am grateful to the BSA for the many friends I have made over the years. I have made dear friends of both adults and youths. I have remained in contact with them and depended on them while going through challenges of my own. I have been able to support them through trials and accompany them during significant events also. They have been anchors in my life.

Participation in the various adventures of the Boy Scouts builds character and enables good decision making. It provides young men with a better perspective of situations and life. Young men have discovered more about themselves, their likes and dislikes, their abilities, and the things they need to improve. Confidence has grown and fear has been contained. Some have discovered what employment to pursue, while others have discovered the joys of service. One treasure is known for sure: All have become better people by their participation in the program, both youths and adults.

A Call to Arms: Suggestions for Improving Society

We can't sit idly by and do nothing if we know there is a problem. According to my research, there is a problem in society with degrading values. Of course, we don't need research studies to tell us this. There are indicators all around us. We can see the increasing amount of violence in this country, and crimes are getting more heinous. Imagine what conditions will be like in ten to twenty years or even fifty. Will our children or their children have any chance at a normal life? It's time to stand up and be counted. It's time to do something before it's too late.

If you're reading this book and you're a youth, enroll in scouting, become a participant, and acquire skills and values to be a better individual.

If you're planning on joining the military for your career, enroll in scouting and become an Eagle Scout. When you join the military, you will advance one rank automatically.

If you're reading this book and you're an adult, sign up and become a volunteer. Help improve the values of the younger generation.

If you're reading this book and you're a father, sign up and become a volunteer, participate with your son and better your relationship, and contribute to the improvement of a troop.

If you're reading this book and you're a craftsman, sign up and become a merit badge counselor.

If you're reading this book and you're a CEO, COO, or other important person at a company, donate money to the BSA or sponsor a BSA troop and make the world a better place.

If you're reading this book and you're a businessman or corporate manager looking for employees, hire a scout or former scout. Look at the list of character traits and skills that a scout acquires and ask yourself if those are some skills that you would want in your employees.

If you're a senator, representative, mayor, governor, or politician, do what you can to support or encourage the BSA in your constituency. Just look at the improvements it develops in people and weigh that against the alternative.

In addition, we can all be better people, friendlier, more helpful, and more concerned for the welfare of other people. Let's do our part to combat the disease in our society. The Boy Scouts of America can help us find the cure.

Receiving Spiritual Guidance: The Rest of the Story

In the introduction I wrote a little bit about the enlightenment I experienced in relation to my scouting time in California, and I'd like to provide the rest of the story. I belong to the Church of Jesus Christ of Latter-day Saints, which encourages its members to seek and obtain personal spiritual guidance. They teach that anyone can receive this guidance from our heavenly father if sought. I strongly believe I have received spiritual guidance many times during my life because when I look back at the outcomes of the choices I have made based on that guidance, I have achieved significant happiness, joy, or success. Some of those times include going on a mission, going to college, moving to California, reflecting on my time in California serving in scouting, and writing this book. It's hard for me to describe how grateful and blessed I feel for having had those experiences.

In my church, it's a tradition that nineteen-year-old young men go on a two-year mission. Serving a mission isn't mandatory, but it is strongly encouraged. For me, I questioned going on a mission, and I suspect that most nineteen-year-old young men do. I thought about sacrificing two years of my life and putting my aspirations on hold. I didn't want to go on a mission, and I was looking for every excuse not to go. But I also felt it was the right thing to do, and I didn't want to disappoint my family. It was at that point of internal conflict that I felt an impression, a thought, or an encouragement to go. It was a strong impression, so strong that whenever I had doubts about going, I was reminded of how strongly I felt encouraged to go. I became determined to go, made all the preparations, and went.

Much of the success I've had in my life was a result of the things I learned going on that mission. I have benefited much more from serving than I would have staying home. By having to live on my own for two years, I learned how to live with someone else, how to take care of myself, how to budget my money, how to work through problems, and how to seek and obtain spiritual guidance.

After returning home from my mission, I thought I would start a business fixing cars. Growing up, most of the work I had done was fixing cars. In junior high, I took a class on small engine repair. In high school, I took vocational auto mechanic classes for two years and an online auto mechanics course that included automatic transmission rebuilds. I was selected to represent our high school in a statewide competition, and we took sixth place. I was always working on someone's car, either mine, my friends, or a neighbor's. Anyway, I thought I would be an auto mechanic. As I started looking for a building to rent, I realized that I needed to go to college.

Going to college had been never on my mind; my parents had never discussed it and, to be honest, I didn't think I was good enough to attend college. But I kept getting these impressions that I should go to college. Since I wanted to run an auto mechanic shop, I thought it would be a good idea to work on a business degree at Utah Tech. I took classes there for a year and did pretty well, but I felt I needed to attend a more significant college and take more science-related classes. I transferred to the University of Utah and enrolled as a computer science student. After one year, I still felt like this wasn't the right pursuit for me. I talked to one of the computer science professors and he suggested electrical engineering. That sounded right, so I transferred into that program the next year. Being in electrical engineering was fun and exciting to me, and I felt like that was what I was supposed to be doing.

After college, I was hired by National Semiconductor and worked there for five years before I was laid off. Before I had even left the building on the day I was let go, I had a job offer from a company in California with which I had been working on a project that designs and builds integrated circuit testers. I wasn't interested in moving to California, so I turned down the offer.

As part of the layoff package, I was able to attend a seminar to help me find a new job. A headhunter received a list of the laid-off engineers and was informing them of some opportunities. I received a call from him about a job in Sacramento, California. I told him I wasn't interested. He told me to just go and check it out, because if I received an offer and didn't like what I saw, I simply could turn it down. Well, I went and liked it. My wife, Julie, was not excited to move to California. Therefore, I called the company and told them I wouldn't go. They paid for my wife and me to go out for a few days so we could see what it was like. They hooked us up with a real estate agent who drove us around looking at houses, schools, and communities. My wife was still concerned about moving, but I started to warm up to the idea.

While we were in Sacramento looking around, the company scheduled a dinner for us at the Cliff House restaurant in Folsom along the American River. We were shocked to find a table full of executives from the company. Most of them were people with whom I had interviewed a couple of weeks previously. It turned out that four of them were section managers and one of them was the VP of the division. Afterward, I felt this was the right choice, not because of the way they had treated us, but because I had another strong impression that we needed to accept this offer and move to Sacramento. I wasn't convinced that my wife was ready to move, but she reassured me that she thought it was the right thing to do even though she was nervous about doing it.

Moving to California, working for Level One/Intel, and participating in scouting were some of the most rewarding things I have ever done, and we made so many close friends. My wife and I have been away from California for almost eight years, and even today we receive dozens of messages weekly from friends we met there. When they are here, we set up visits, go to dinner, or rendezvous at a state park.

As for my scouting experiences, I have hiked all over the hills in California in every season of the year. I have canoed many of the lakes and rivers, some of them dozens of times. I have met some of the most dedicated men in scouting that you could imagine. I have never seen people sacrifice so much. They have been great examples to me, and they have provided a lifetime's worth of adventures for me and my family in twelve years.

My time in California was complete, thanks to my employment at Level One/Intel. My responsibility was to write test programs to test the communication types of integrated circuits. It was a fun job—challenging, fast paced, cutting edge, and difficult, but rewarding as well. I was able to provide some great engineering work for those companies that generated or saved them millions of dollars. Over the years, I was fortunate to work on some significant projects. Decades of employment in this field has brought joy and happiness as well as financial stability.

I would ride my bicycle to and from work usually three times a week. The distance was 17.3 miles, so this was around one hundred miles a week. I used to keep track of my distance on a yearly basis, and I biked an average of 4,500 miles a year. A couple of years, I managed to travel as many as 5,200 to 5,400 miles. I had a Spinergy wheel that was rebuilt three times over the years. I've retired it, since the wheel is so old I can't get parts for it anymore. I would imagine that it has over 70,000 miles on it. Half of the path I followed from my house to work was along the bike trail of the American River. You can imagine how familiar that bike trail was to me after riding six to seven hours a week along it for more than twelve years.

Many of our family vacations were spent enjoying locations around the state, such as Disneyland, Yosemite, Lassen, Bodega Bay, Dillon's Beach, San Francisco, and the Sierras. Around northern California are gold mining state parks that were fun to visit. Some used high-pressure water to erode the landscape, while others dug up the dirt and used water to process it. At Columbia State Park, dirt is dug up and processed with a sluice box. When we visited there, the curator took a shovel, dug up a bucketful of dirt right were we stood, ran it through a sluice box, and found gold. California has so many things to see and do that you would never get tired of the adventure there. When we moved back to Utah, it took a little getting used to. Everyone was friendly and helpful, but there was something different about living in Utah versus living in California. I felt like I had left home. Many mornings after waking up, I would lay in bed reflecting on all the great experiences we'd had in California. Many times, the focus was on scouting adventures. One morning, I felt like I should make a record of all the things I had learned from scouting or what I had seen a scout learn from scouting. Again, it felt like I was inspired or compelled to record this information.

In my church, we are taught to seek inspiration or guidance by pondering or reflecting on a situation or concern. We are taught to study a situation in our mind and what we think we should do, and ask in prayer if our conclusion is the right decision. If we have studied a scripture, then we are encouraged to study it out in our minds for understanding. When I have followed this advice, many times I have come to a deeper understanding. Somehow, pondering brings deeper understanding.

This was my process as I accumulated a list of all the things I learned from scouting. After accumulating the list, I felt inspired to compile it into a book and get it published. I'm not a good creative writer; I have been trained in technical writing. Therefore, I know for sure it was not my idea to put these ideas into a book. Throughout my life, I have always wanted to benefit the community or the world. I have wanted to give something back, and this book might be one way I can do that. I have seen what a great blessing scouting has been in the lives of young men and me personally. If this book can encourage someone else to enjoy those same benefits, then I will have accomplished that goal.

I have reviewed the times in my life when I have felt significantly that I received guidance from above, and I have come to the conclusion that it must have been exactly that. In many of the situations, I was encouraged to do something I had not considered doing or I was against doing. When I look back at how significantly blessed I have been because I have followed that guidance, I am astounded. In each case, it brought increased happiness, joy, and success; fond memories; and even stronger financial stability. People may consider me crazy or delusional to say I have received inspiration from a heavenly father, but I don't care. It has provided me a happy, enjoyable life.

Appendix A

Research: Positive Youth Development Resource Manual

In support of BSA programs, I referenced the *Positive Youth Development Resource Manual* by Jutta Dotterweich. This manual tries to provide all the information necessary for anyone to teach or encourage a youth to develop positive traits or characteristics. Section 1 indicates that four conditions are required for positive youth development: meeting basic needs (food, clothing, shelter, etc.), preparedness, connectedness, and engagement. A review of the scouting program would suggest that the BSA programs meet all of the last three conditions. Hopefully the first condition is being met by the young man's family. The author of the manual provides hundreds of references in the last fifteen pages for further study.

Summary of Treasures for a Young Man

Acquired Characteristics from Participation in Scouting: Accumulation from Studies and Personal Witness		
High Likelihood to Exercise	Solve Community Problem	Honest
High Likelihood to Boat	High Likelihood to Vote	Respect Property
High Likelihood to Fish	Leader in Workplace	Confident
High Likelihood to Camp	Leader in Community	Seeks to Do His Best
Visit National Park	Environmentally Active	Kind
Satisfied Free Time	Avoid Environmentally Damaging Products	Participate in Extracurricular Activities
Culture	Water Conservation	Thrifty
Play Instrument	Learn Something New	Brave
Book Reading	Continuous Learning (Classes)	Reverent
Close to Family	Achieve Personal Goal	Chaste
Close to Friends	Achieve Spiritual Goal	Take School Seriously
Close to Religion	Achieve Financial Goal	Determined
Close to Coworkers	Prepare for Future (Home)	Helpful
Less Likely to Drink Alcohol	Prepare for Future (Career)	Courteous
Friends with Neighbors	CPR Certified	Obedient
Visit Neighbors	Meeting Place for Emergency	Cheerful
Participation in Club or Groups	Seek to Exceed Expectation	Clean
Spiritual Presence in Nature	Do What's Right	Offer Service
Donate to Church	Work Hard to Get Ahead	Develop Leadership
Donate to Charity	Treat Others with Respect	Loyal
Volunteer Time to Church	Respect Religious Leaders	Mentally Aware
Volunteer Time to Charity	Respect Flag	Good Decision Maker
Work Well in Team Setting	Respect Life	Love of Scouting
Well Grounded	Willing to Do Hard Things	Well-Rounded Character
Concerned for Others	Spiritual Development	Determination
Competence	Reliable	Lack of Entitlement

Summary of Treasures for Adults

Includes All Treasures Listed for Youth
Help Boys Achieve their Potential
Better Communication Abilities
Enhanced Relationships
Spiritual Development
Better Management
Better Organization
Better Parenting
Better Fitness
Better World
Better Understanding
Better Appreciation of Scouting

Research topic	Scout	Non-Scout
Graduate from high school	91%	87%
Graduate from college	35%	19%
Post-graduate degree	10%	6%
Satisfied with personal life	97%	91%
Satisfied with job	83%	73%
Satisfied with American society	52%	54%
Satisfied with world	45%	44%
Family key to happiness	81%	72%
Lifelong friends	89%	74%
Attend church (once per week)	26%	19%
Never attend church	13%	23%
Believe shouldn't through trash out the window	92%	87%
Believe shouldn't exaggerate on resume	79%	66%
Believe should declare all tax	73%	68%
Believe shouldn't keep excess change from store	71%	63%
Believe shouldn't take supplies from work	57%	53%
Should vote	47%	29%
Show concern for neighbor's property	37%	24%
Keep own property clean	28%	23%
Keep informed of current events	26%	21%
Keep physically fit	25%	21%
Attend church services	22%	14%
Donation to religious organization	19%	12%
Participation in youth organization	17%	12%
Participation in charitable organization	15%	10%
Participation in community	13%	11%
Agree scouting helps develop character	99%	89%
Scouting benefit to inner-city children	92%	86%
Scouting and family go together	88%	78%
Participation in sports	75%	72%
Participation in music, drama, or dance	36%	22%
Participation in arts and crafts	29%	21%
Participation in hobbies	39%	29%

Participation in school clubs	27%	19%
Participation in farming and gardening	20%	15%
Participation in yearbook/newspaper	12%	5%
Sees self as confident	58%	42%
Sees self as leader	57%	37%
Sees self as helping other in need	46%	34%
A grades	29%	17%
As & Bs	34%	32%

Table 2: an incomplete list of characteristics indicated from Harris Interactive study

Appendix B

Suggestions for Winter Camp

Okpik-trained leaders	Everyone should attend winter camp training
Use layering system for clothing (no cotton)	Wick for base layer (synthetic/wool)
Fleece for insulation layer (synthetic/wool)	Waterproof, windproof, & breathable shell
Everyone to have a whistle	Someone should know where you went
Tell the family when you expect to be home	Put on dry clothes before bed (including socks)
Wear hat (fleece) to bed	Wear snow boots (like Caribou Sorels)
Build fire hut with fire barrel	Get body parts warm before bed
Earplugs for the noisy bears (snoring adults)	Helpful to have leader with medical experience
Establish rule for boys to stay off frozen lakes or ponds	Follow general rules of BSA, like buddy system
Use igloos or snow caves for shelter	Shelters to have cold sink
Start snow shelters the weekend before	If using snow cave or igloos, plan enough time to build
Shelters need vents for fresh air	Drink lots of water
Eat hot foods as much as possible	Keep pot of hot water available for drinks
Add butter or margarine to foods	Can use cardboard oven
Use 0 degree sleeping bag (no Coleman bags)	Use cardboard below sleeping bag
Sleeping pad	Can use solar blanket below sleeping bag
Can use fleece sleeping bag liner	Bring a first aid kit
Use fire barrel during winter camps	Bring extra sleeping bags, tarps, and rope

Suggestions for Backpack Trips

Backpacker Awareness–trained leaders	Backpacker training for troop before event
Generate plan with TOPO	Use GPS if possible
Remove shoes and socks to walk through steams	Use walkie-talkies if possible
Food focus on lightweight/dehydration	Water filtration/purification
Drink lots of water	Suggest use of hydration pack
Can use backpack stoves to cook food	Can bring backpack oven to share with troop
Bear bag food if required	Bring pepper spray for bears if needed
Follow general rules of BSA, like buddy system	Take head count after hikes
Use tube tent if possible	Use bare essential clothing
Use layered clothing system	Suggest nylon pants with zip-off leggings
Suggest lightweight hiking shoes already broken in	Backpack 25% of body weight
Evaluate boys pre-hikes	Participants should have physical before trip
First aid kit with lots of mole skin	>90% deet mosquito repellent
Sunscreen	Someone should know where you went
Tell the family when you expect to be home	Everyone to have a whistle
Sleeping bag should be lightweight mummy	Can use solar blanket below sleeping bag

Suggestions for a Well-Run Troop

Charter organization to support troop with funds and Leadership
Charter organization to support troop by keeping unit leaders for years
Unit leaders to attend BSA trainings
Unit leaders to attend roundtable
Parents attend troop committee meetings
Parents assigned position on troop committee
Parents to support troop with attendance at troop activities
Troop run by youth leadership
Youth attend junior leader training
Youth hold troop planning meeting on regular basis
Youth plan a variety of activities
Yearly winter camp
Should plan 50-mile trip every other year
Weekly activities should have challenge/game/entertainment
Joint other troops for activities
Take pictures of activities and present a slide show at court of honor
Use achievement tracking software for youth advancement
Make sure to recognize youth achievements and advancements

Suggestions for Further Reading

Brunson, Austin. *Moral Responsibility in a Rapidly Declining Society.* http://bigthink.com/articles/moral-responsibility-in-a-rapidly-declining-society

Fisher, Pete. *The Decline of Morality in Our Society.* http://www.renewamerica.com/columns/fisher/051005

Gawkins, Michael J., and Robert Connolly. Reversing Decades of Societal Degradation in America. Carlisle, PA: U.S. Army War College Civilian Research Project, 2012.

Harris Interactive. *Values of Americans: A Study of Ethics and Character.* Rochester, NY: Boy Scouts of America Youth and Family Research Center, 2005.

Harris Interactive. *Values of Scouts—A Study of Ethics and Character.* Rochester, NY: Boy Scouts of America Youth and Family Research Center, 2005.

Jang, Sung J., Byron R. Johnson, and Young-Il Kim. *Eagle Scouts Merit Beyond the Badge.* Waco, Texas: Baylor University, 2012.

Kasser, Tim. The High Price of Materialism. Cambridge: MIT Press, 1993.

I would instruct my readers to do their own searches for similar articles using the following search text: "Declining values in America."

About the Author

My name is Jeff Johnson. I was born in Provo, Utah, on June 13, 1960, to Bette and Merlin Johnson. I was the second oldest of five siblings. My dad was an architect and liked checking out new places to live, so we lived in a few places when I was growing up. It seemed like we moved every year or two. We moved to Portland, Oregon, when I was three and to San Francisco when I was five. When we moved to new places it felt like we were on vacation because my parents would take us around to check out the interesting attractions. Eventually we moved back to Utah, where I graduated from high school.

From January 1980 to January 1982, I went on a mission for our church to Missouri and Illinois. Upon my return, I started college at Utah Tech and majored in business. About this time I met my wife, Julie Layton, and we were married in August 1983. After a year at Utah Tech I transferred to the University of Utah and majored in computer science before switching a year later to electrical engineering, which is the degree I graduated with in 1989. My focus was mostly on microwave technology, basically high-frequency radio wave technology. I had three job offers right out of college—two out of state and one in state. I turned down the jobs at Ford Aerospace and at the navy radar systems group and took the in-state job with National Semiconductor in West Jordan, Utah.

I worked at National Semiconductor writing programs to test memory chips. This lasted five years before I was laid off and my family and I moved to California so I could take a job with Level One Communications. Employment for Level One consisted of writing programs and designing hardware to test a communications type of integrated circuit. Five years later, Intel Corporation bought the company and I worked for them for another eight years. While working at Level One, I applied to get into the master's program at CSU in communications. This was the electrical engineering type of communications, such as cell phone networks, wireless signals, microwave communications, and optical communications. I got into the program and graduated in 2003. In 2007, we moved back to Utah.

I have been asked to work in scouting from the time I was married until now. I have had a position in scouting for all of those years, give or take eight months. That's more than thirty years of almost continuous volunteer work in scouting. I have been to every training course except one that the BSA offers, many of them several times. The only exception is Philmont Scout Ranch, and I hope to get there someday. I have been on several teams that have provided unit leader training. I have been to dozens of scout camps and hundreds of troop overnighters and probably close to one thousand weekday activities. I hope to share how scouting has blessed my life far more than anything I have done for scouting.

www.ingramcontent.com/pod-product-compliance
Lightning Source LLC
LaVergne TN
LVHW021509080426
835509LV00018B/2457